METHODIST
MISSION
AT 200

"Come and see God's deeds." (Psalm 66:5 CEB)

To all those missionaries and mission agency workers whose stories are included here, and to all those whose stories are waiting to be told.

METHODIST MISSION
AT 200

Serving Faithfully
Amid the Tensions

Edited by:
Thomas Kemper & David W. Scott

Abingdon Press™
Nashville

METHODIST MISSION AT 200:
SERVING FAITHFULLY AMID THE TENSIONS

ISBN: 9781791015985

Chapter 2 originally appeared in a slightly different form in *Methodist History* 58, no. 1 & 2, Mission Bicentennial Double Issue, Oct. 2019/Jan. 2020.

20 21 22 23 24 25 26 27 28 29—10 9 8 7 6 5 4 3 2 1
MANUFACTURED IN THE UNITED STATES OF AMERICA

CONTENTS

INTRODUCTION

METHODIST MISSION AT 200

David W. Scott and Thomas Kemper

This book commemorates 200 years of Methodist mission history. In 2019, the General Board of Global Ministries of The United Methodist Church celebrated the 200th anniversary of its founding as the first denomination-wide mission agency of Methodism in the United States. But the story of Methodist mission and Global Ministries starts a few years before the organization was founded, with a man named John Stewart.

John Stewart, missionary to the Wyandot, 1816–1823. This sketch was drawn by Rev. N. B. C. Love in 1889, depicting Stewart's northwestern journey to the Wyandot nation. Housed in John Stewart United Methodist Church lobby display, Upper Sandusky, Ohio. *Photo: Dale Devene Jr., courtesy of Betsy Bowen.*

John Stewart and the Founding of the Missionary Society

John Stewart was a free African American who, in 1816, sensed God's call and responded by going as a self-appointed missionary evangelist to the Wyandot[1] native people living on their Grand Reserve in what is now Upper Sandusky, Ohio. Working with Wyandot leaders, Stewart's preaching and singing eventually found a good response, and he formed a Methodist community among the Wyandot, the first Native American Methodist congregation.

Although he began as a self-appointed missionary, John Stewart eventually sought and received recognition of his ministry by being commissioned as a local preacher by the Mad River quarterly conference of the Ohio Annual Conference of the Methodist Episcopal Church. With this recognition, word of the success of Stewart's work spread in Ohio and throughout the United States. In response, the Ohio conference eventually sent ordained clergy as additional missionaries to support Stewart's work.

That news traveled to New York City as well, then one of the hubs of Methodist organizational activity in the US. There, word of the work of John Stewart inspired Methodist leaders to establish the first denomination-wide missionary organization. On April 5, 1819, Nathan Bangs, Freeborn Garrettson, Joshua Soule, and other leading figures of Methodism met to establish the Missionary Society of the Methodist Episcopal Church, the earliest predecessor of today's General Board of Global Ministries of The United Methodist Church.[2]

Some in the Methodist connection at that time thought that a missionary society was not necessary, since the "whole system [of Methodism] is a missionary system."[3] Yet Bangs and the other leaders recognized that there was a need for an organization that could give special attention to fostering relationships and collaboration across annual conferences, that could organize the resources necessary to carry out the church's missionary calling, and that could respond as it discerned the Spirit calling the church into mission in new places and new forms.

---

1.   The name is variously spelled *Wyandot, Wyandott,* and *Wyandotte.* In this book, *Wyandot* is used to refer to the historical group with whom Stewart ministered, and *Wyandotte* is used to refer to their present-day descendants.

2.   For a complete list of predecessor organizations to Global Ministries, see appendix A.

3.   Quoted in Wade Crawford Barclay, *History of Methodist Missions,* part 1, *Early American Methodism 1769–1844,* vol. 1, *Missionary Motivation and Expansion* (New York: The Board of Missions and Church Extension of The Methodist Church, 1949), 206.

Rev. Nathan Bangs, one of the founders of the Missionary Society of the Methodist Episcopal Church.
Engraving: Published at the Methodist Book Room, 200 Mulberry Street, New York. Painted by Paradise. Engraved by E. Mackensie.
Engraved Portraits of the First Methodist Divines, Archives and Manuscript Department, Pitts Theology Library, Emory University.

Bangs cited six motivations for starting the organization. Two concerned financial considerations and one was sociological—keeping up with what other denominations were doing. The other three lay out an interesting missional rationale: (1) reaching people on the remote western frontier of the young United States; (2) ministry with Native Americans; and (3) extension of mission "to more distant fields" (that is, abroad). Bangs noted, "We take the liberty of observing that our [religious] views are not restricted to our own nation or colour." In short, the Missionary Society was intended to enlarge the reach of the gospel to persons and groups not already served or not well-served by the church, to offer them Christ, and to accompany them on their faith journeys. Moreover, the Missionary Society was initially predicated on the recognition that the truth of the gospel transcends race, nation, and ethnicity—that all persons are equally children of God.[4]

The next year, Bangs and his fellow workers brought their plans for the new organization before the General Conference, recognizing that if the Missionary Society was to serve the whole church, it must be affirmed by the whole church through the General Conference. Bishop McKendree commended the Missionary Society in his address that opened that General Conference, and the proposal was sent to committee. After reviewing the matter, the Committee on Missions came back with a report that said,

> Methodism itself is a Missionary system. Yield the Missionary spirit, and you yield the very life-blood of the cause. . . . With these views, [the committee] submit the following. . . . That this Conference do highly approve of the institution of the Missionary Society, of the Methodist Episcopal

---

4. Barclay, *History of Methodist Missions*, 206.

Church, in the city of New York and, on the recommendation of the Managers thereof, do agree to, and adopt the following Constitution.[5]

On May 26, 1820, General Conference overwhelmingly voted to recognize the Missionary Society. Methodists recognized then, as we still recognize now, that organizing our relationships and resources for mission into a formal agency is an expression of, not an abdication of, the missionary nature of our faith and the responsibility of each Christian and each Christian community to participate in the *missio Dei*.

Story, Theology, Connection, and Tension

When looked at one way, the Missionary Society was created because people were inspired by listening to the stories of other faithful Christians in mission. This is perhaps appropriate for Christians, whose faith is rooted in the story of Jesus and his mission on earth. But the power of story to inspire and motivate is worth noting. A recognition of the power of story stands at the heart of this volume. This book is an attempt to share a few of the stories that have shaped Methodist mission history, starting with John Stewart and the Wyandot; to explain how the power of these stories and the lessons drawn from them have shaped Global Ministries and the work it does; and to invite you, the reader, to be moved and motivated by these stories as well.

While story is the root of this book, theology represents the branches, leaves, and fruit. The lessons drawn from stories of mission past and present often grow into and take the form of theological convictions about mission. As faithful Christians observe what God has done and is doing in the world, they are able to discern theological truths about God's mission. And those truths then feed back into the choices that people make as they live out the story of God's mission. In short, there is a close connection between story and theology. This book, then, builds theology upon story by using some of the stories of Methodist mission over the past 200 years to bear witness to the lessons those stories offer about God's mission.

This act of combining story and theology is nothing new for Global Ministries. The agency has long supported taking what it has learned from mission

---

5. Quoted in Barclay, *History of Methodist Missions*, 211.

and articulating it in the form of theological reflections. Global Ministries first adopted an official theology of mission statement, entitled "Partnership in God's Mission," in October 1986.[6] That initial statement was revised and rewritten in 2011. Directors and members of the United Methodist Missionary Association were active in producing several drafts, and the final version, approved by the directors, is now widely used. You will find references to what Global Ministries now simply calls its "Theology of Mission statement" throughout this book, and a complete copy is included in appendix B.

Stories imply connection—between the storyteller and the listener and between those sharing the story and the characters in the story. Thus, it is appropriate that an emphasis on connection is another major feature of this book—connection between people, between organizations, between various forms of mission work. Global Ministries often speaks of its work as "connecting the church in mission." It is able to do so because of the wealth of relationships it has built up over 200 years—relationships that cross boundaries of geography, race, gender, nation, even denomination—as it partners with United Methodists and historically affiliated Methodist and uniting churches throughout the world, including our important partnerships with United Methodist Women and other agencies. Sometimes these relationships look like formal partnerships between organizations, but much more often, they look like something more personal—like friendship. This book is both a sharing of the fruits of the relationships that have undergirded the mission of United Methodists and their predecessors over the past two centuries and an invitation to continue to be in relationship with Global Ministries.

Befitting a book that highlights partnership, this book is itself a result of partnership. While we (Thomas Kemper and David Scott) served as editors for the book and, along with Arun Jones, wrote most of the content, the book represents the contributions of many people. Elliott Wright, long-term staff writer and information officer of Global Ministries, contributed significant drafting and research to many chapters of the book. Glenn Kellum arranged the sidebar stories and quotes that serve to illustrate the themes of each chapter, each of which represents another person who contributed to the book. Those quoted in the sidebars graciously agreed to share their words. Christie House coordinated the process of identifying the wonderful pictures that serve to bring the stories in the book to life, with assistance from

---

6. "Partnership in God's Mission: Theology of Mission Statement" (New York: General Board of Global Ministries, 1986).

Jennifer Silver and Anthony Trueheart. Glenn Kellum, Christie House, and Mary Lou Boice provided extensive feedback on the book. Margaret Fenton Lebeck, Izabel Scott, and others at Global Ministries also played important roles in moving this book forward. The book is also a product of a partnership between Global Ministries and The United Methodist Publishing House.

Of course, neither stories nor relationships are simple. Good stories are driven by a sense of conflict or tension. And there are tensions in the choices that must be made in telling stories—how to frame them, what parts to include and what parts to omit, with whom to share them, and so on. Moreover, there are tensions within even the healthiest of relationships, and relationships experience the stress of outside tensions and turmoil that affect one or more partner. While such tensions can at times be destructive, they can also lead to great growth in a relationship. Thus, a fourth major feature of this book, as indicated in the subtitle, is recognition of the tensions that have characterized mission historically and still characterize mission today. These tensions are not problems that must be solved, but rather they are truths that must be recognized and even appreciated for how they help move the story of mission forward and how they help us as Christians grow in our faith and our relationship with God.

Overview of the Book

This book is titled *Methodist Mission at 200*. As previously noted, it was written on the occasion of Global Ministries' 200th anniversary and because of that anniversary. Yet the book is not about Methodist mission *over the course of* 200 years. It is about Methodist mission *at* 200. Thus the book is not primarily concerned with summarizing or providing an overview of the last 200 years of Methodist mission history. Instead, it is a reflection on how Global Ministries understands itself and its work after two centuries. This self-understanding is informed by the past, derived from the agency's theology, and oriented toward its future. This book is primarily a work about theology and how that theology shapes practice, not a historical work, though that theology and practice are heavily shaped by the lessons of history.

The first chapter, written by David W. Scott, delves further into the bicentennial as an occasion for reflection by the agency. It presents the thinking by Global Ministries and its staff and partners who planned the celebration of the bicentennial of Methodist mission. It explores a series of questions that planners brought to that work as they sought to faithfully honor what had come before in a way that emphasized how Methodists understand mission now.

The second and third chapters look at stories from Methodist mission past for the sake of drawing lessons about the ongoing nature of Methodist mission. The second chapter of this book, written by Arun W. Jones, examines in greater depth the story of John Stewart, identifying a series of three tensions in Stewart's work that also characterize all mission work. The body of that chapter comes from the keynote speech given by Jones at the opening banquet of "Answering the Call: Hearing God's Voice in Methodist Mission Past, Present, and Future," the Methodist Mission Bicentennial Conference, held April 8–10, 2019, in Atlanta, Georgia, and cosponsored by Global Ministries and Candler School of Theology of Emory University. The speech is prefaced by an original introduction written for this volume. The third chapter, written by David W. Scott, looks at the sweep of the 200 years since Stewart's work, and reflects on some characteristics of that work that continue to be true of Methodist mission today.

The fourth and fifth chapters, both written by Thomas Kemper, present the theology that has guided Global Ministries (and its component organization UMCOR, the United Methodist Committee on Relief) over the past ten years and recounts how that theology has shaped the agency's actions in that time. The fourth chapter looks at three themes in mission theology—mission as the *missio Dei*, collaboration, and facilitation—and how those themes informed the mission work Global Ministries has done with others. The fifth chapter explores the relationship between mission and diakonia, or service, especially as it informs the relationship between Global Ministries and UMCOR.

The sixth chapter, written by David W. Scott, unites the themes of historical reflection and recent mission practice by returning to the story of John Stewart and the Wyandotte. After briefly reviewing the scope of Wyandotte and Methodist history since the time of John Stewart, it shares the story of the recent resumption of close relationships between the Wyandotte people and the people called Methodist, especially in Upper Sandusky, Ohio, but extending to Global Ministries and United Methodists throughout Ohio and the world.

A brief concluding epilogue by Thomas Kemper looks to the future of mission by laying forth four enduring tensions that characterize mission now and will continue to be part of mission practice as Methodists continue to answer God's call to mission.

Throughout, the text of the chapters is illustrated with a series of sidebars that present remarks made at the bicentennial conference in Atlanta in 2019, biographies of Methodists who have served in mission, remarks by those involved in the relationship between the Methodists and the Wyandotte, news stories, and other material that provides additional perspectives on the themes of the text. This material aims both to further connect the reflections in the main text to specific stories, past and present, and to expand upon the element of collaboration and partnership in the book. A series of appendices offers further details on elements related to the main body of the text.

We hope you will find this book both interesting and spiritually edifying—that it informs but also uplifts and inspires, as together the church seeks to faithfully answer God's call, encouraged by the stories of those who have come before us, conscious of the tensions that surround us, and dependent upon the relationships that connect us.

CHAPTER 1

CELEBRATING THE BICENTENNIAL OF METHODIST MISSION

David W. Scott

As Global Ministries began to prepare to commemorate its bicentennial, the question arose: How should the agency celebrate its bicentennial in a way that draws upon what Methodists have learned from the past two centuries of Methodist mission history and acknowledges the theological convictions with which the organization operates? This chapter shares some of the scope of that celebration, but more importantly, it shows how those plans reflected answers to a series of questions with which Global Ministries staff and partners wrestled as we sought to design a celebration that was true to the organization today, true to those who had served faithfully over the years before, and true to the God who calls all of us into mission.

Components of the Celebration

The bicentennial included three main initiatives. Leading into the bicentennial year, Global Ministries solicited mission stories from around the world to help reveal, make available, and memorialize the history of mission in all its forms. The stories about mission came from scholarly sources, archives, congregations, conferences, and individuals, and reflected the diversity of mission voices and the range of people worldwide who have devoted their lives to mission. To make these stories accessible, Global Ministries launched a website in 2017: www.methodistmission200.org.

Participants gather for "Answering the Call: Hearing God's Voice in Methodist Mission Past, Present, and Future," the Methodist Mission Bicentennial Conference, Atlanta, Georgia, April 8-10, 2019.
Photo: Jennifer Silver, Global Ministries

The bicentennial also included a world conference, held April 8–10, 2019, entitled "Answering the Call: Hearing God's Voice in Methodist Mission Past, Present, and Future." The conference was cosponsored by Global Ministries and Candler School of Theology of Emory University and was held in Atlanta, Georgia. The dates were chosen to closely coincide with the 200th anniversary of the founding of the Missionary Society on April 5, 1819. Over 250 people from throughout the world attended this conference.

Finally, the bicentennial included an intentional strategy of partnering with annual conferences, local churches, United Methodist Communications, the Commission on the General Conference, and other United Methodist entities to share the story of United Methodist mission and its history at a wide variety of events and venues over the course of several years, from 2018 through the rescheduled General Conference in 2021.

Celebrating an Organization and Celebrating the *Missio Dei*

While the description of these three initiatives is relatively simple, it takes a bit more recounting to explain how the organization arrived at the details of this celebration. That process was shaped by three questions with which the bicentennial planners wrestled and one goal that we tried to pursue. In their own way, each of these questions represents a tension amid which those who planned the bicentennial tried to serve faithfully.

The first question planners asked was, How do you celebrate a milestone for a particular United Methodist mission organization (Global Ministries) while recognizing that mission is the *missio Dei* and extends far beyond the work of any one organization? This question was the ground for a host of related questions: How should the affiliated autonomous Methodist and united churches, who are an important part of Methodist mission history, be included in the celebration? How should Global Ministries partner with other United Methodist general agencies or denominational groups, acknowledging that they, too, have roles in God's mission? In particular, how could the bicentennial acknowledge the historical ties and ongoing partnerships between Global Ministries and United Methodist Women? It was exciting that the year 2019 also marked the 150th anniversary of the Woman's Foreign Missionary Society (WFMS) of the Methodist Episcopal Church, the earliest forerunner of today's United Methodist Women (UMW).

The first answer to these questions was, of course, partnership. The bicentennial celebration was not something that Global Ministries could or should do alone. Indeed, the very first meeting that I (David) attended for the sake of planning the bicentennial happened not at Global Ministries' headquarters, but at the offices of the General Commission on Archives and History (GCAH). GCAH, UMW, the General Board of Higher Education and Ministry (GBHEM), the General Council on Finance and Administration (GCFA), United Methodist Communications, and others were important partners throughout the process, and their staff and expertise were essential to the project. Rev. Fred Day, General Secretary of GCAH, and Dr. Amos Nascimento, Associate General Secretary of GBHEM, both served on the planning committee. Harriett Olson, General Secretary of United Methodist Women, was an invaluable conversation partner and collaborator throughout. Dr. Dale Patterson of GCAH was also an enormous help.

3

Bishops throughout the connection, as well as Directors of Connectional Ministry and other conference staff, were also key partners. They helped share messages about the bicentennial, invited Global Ministries' leadership to present about Methodist mission history, and submitted stories about their conferences' involvement with mission. Bishop Thomas Bickerton of the New York Episcopal Area served as chair of the bicentennial planning committee, in recognition of New York as the original home of the Missionary Society.

Photo: Jennifer Silver, Global Ministries

"We are thrilled at the invitation we received from Thomas Kemper and David Scott to co-host this event. . . . Candler School of Theology is strengthened in having such a remarkable local partner in global missions. We were gratified that the excellent faculty and other resources of our school were part of the calculation of the General Board of Global Ministries in its move to Atlanta. We partnered productively with the board in NYC, but now the opportunities have expanded to the benefit of both. We're delighted."

—*Dr. Jan Love, dean, Candler School of Theology, at the Methodist Mission Bicentennial Conference, Atlanta, April 2019, opening banquet*

Global Ministries partnered with seminaries as well. Candler School of Theology of Emory University and its dean, Dr. Jan Love, were of course essential partners as cohosts of the conference. Rev. Dr. Arun W. Jones of

Candler, Dr. Dana L. Robert of Boston University School of Theology, and Rev. Dr. Luther Oconer of United Theological Seminary all served on the bicentennial steering committee. Through Dana Robert's assistance, the Center for Global Christianity and Mission at Boston University was an essential resource in both initially developing the online story collection and in ensuring that the materials collected will have a place in perpetuity as part of their History of Missiology online collection.[1]

There were other collaborators, too. Pastors, congregations, professors, nonprofit leaders, and everyday United Methodists sent in stories from around the world of the faithful Christians in mission who had made the biggest impact on their lives. People submitted stories from Africa, Asia, Europe, Latin America, and North America. And none of the work of the bicentennial could have happened without strong internal collaboration within Global Ministries, with people working across departments and often outside the scope of their normal duties. I am very grateful for the way in which the entire organization pulled together on this project.

Another way in which Global Ministries sought to recognize the scope of the *missio Dei*, even as it celebrated its own organizational milestone, was to look at the broad scope of Methodist and Evangelical United Brethren mission history when collecting stories. Thus, the stories include figures that served in various places, engaged in a variety of forms of mission, and had a range of relationships with the denominations and structures of Methodism. That means the story collection includes not only stories of those who worked for or were missionaries of Global Ministries, but also predecessor denominations and agencies, including women's agencies, and even figures (like John Stewart!) that were never formally missionaries or employees of Global Ministries and its predecessors. This is not an attempt to appropriate others' stories. Global Ministries is not, for instance, trying to take credit for the work that intrepid WFMS missionaries did, sometimes despite interference from the male-run mission board. Rather, the inclusion of these stories is instead an attempt to recognize that Global Ministries and its predecessors have no monopoly on mission, and furthermore to humbly learn how God has moved across and beyond organizational boundaries.

---

1. See Methodist Mission Bicentennial category, Boston University School of Theology History of Missiology website: http://www.bu.edu/missiology/category/methodist-mission -bicentennial/.

Just some of the over 1,000 performers involved in "The Wayfarer," a drama presented at the Methodist Mission Centenary, July 1919, Columbus, Ohio Wayfarer Pageant—"Halleluyia Trumpeters"
Photo: GCAH Mission Photograph Album - MISC #4, P. 123

Celebration and Repentance

Another question with which event organizers wrestled was how to celebrate the successes of Methodist mission past while recognizing the shortcomings in terms of racism, sexism, colonialism, and other failings. In this regard, I often thought about the Mission Centenary celebration in 1919. By some metrics, the Mission Centenary was an astounding undertaking. Between the Methodist Episcopal Church and Methodist Episcopal Church, South, the Centenary raised the contemporary equivalent of 2 billion dollars for mission. Over a million people attended a "World's Fair" of Methodist mission, held over three weeks in the summer of 1919 in Columbus, Ohio. There were also massive prayer and evangelism campaigns associated with the Centenary. It was clear that the bicentennial celebration would have nothing close to the same magnitude.

Yet despite the big numbers associated with the Mission Centenary, from the current historical vantage point, one can see that it was a flawed celebration, shot through with racist, classist, nationalist, and colonialist assumptions about mission. The cover of the bulletin for the Centenary World's Fair showed a middle-class white American who was literally above everyone else—the working class, immigrants, ethnic minorities, indigenous people, and people from other countries. That pretty much summed up the attitude of the times. Well-to-do white Americans saw themselves as the saviors of the world, and salvation meant becoming like well-to-do white Americans. The Centenary was awash in American triumphalism, racism, and sense of superiority. It was clear that bicentennial planners wanted the bicentennial celebration to be very different in tone.

• •

"It was clear from the first moments of the Bicentennial Conference in Atlanta that this event would bear little resemblance to the church's centenary celebrations of 1919. 'Answering the Call: Hearing God's Voice in Methodist Mission Past, Present and Future,' the theme of the bicentennial celebration, encouraged participants to listen to present voices, reflect on 200 years of mission practice and discern God's guidance in reshaping mission ministry for its third century of service. The centenary, by contrast, described as Methodism's 'World's Fair,' spanned three weeks and drew more than a million visitors, celebrating the great progress and scope of American Methodist mission. . . . Bishop Hee-Soo Jung . . . welcomed visitors and acknowledged the intrinsic differences of this postcolonial gathering to the mindsets and perspectives of the missionaries it celebrated, sent out in the early years of Methodist mission societies. 'We now see a paradigm shift to transformative partnerships, empowering and life-giving connections.'"

—*Christie R. House, "Bicentennial of Methodist Mission—a Time for Connection and Reflection," Global Ministries Communications, April 12, 2019*

• •

Thus, rather than try to emulate the Centenary's attitude of triumphalism, planners sought instead to practice attitudes of humility, listening, and learning. As Global Ministries sought out partners, it tried to be invitational rather than commanding in forming partnerships. Of course, learning does not only mean willingness to learn from past mistakes. It also means the opportunity to learn about the amazing positive accomplishments of Method-

ists in mission. I was repeatedly inspired by the stories in the bicentennial story collection of Methodists in mission who had done amazing things for God.

A bicentennial conference participant observes posters presenting stories of notable Methodist mission figures.
Photo: Jennifer Silver, Global Ministries

The bicentennial conference, too, sought to balance celebration of accomplishment and acknowledgement of shortcomings over the past 200 years. The academic component of the conference, with its panels of papers on various mission topics, was an opportunity to reflect critically on Methodist mission history. The conference also displayed posters of stories of great Methodist mission heroes. (For a list of those posters, see appendix C.) Worship at the conference sought to celebrate mission and mission partnership in the opening banquet, acknowledge pain from past mistakes and unresolved problems in the world, and move toward recommitment to mission through a remembrance of baptism ceremony at the closing.

Margins, Center, and Everywhere

The third and final question with which bicentennial planners wrestled was how to recognize the importance of mission from the margins and mission from everywhere to everywhere when doing so from a geographic and organizational center. Relatedly, how could Global Ministries, as a center of institutional, denominational, and financial power headquartered in the United States, acknowledge that mission is the work of the whole church throughout the world?

• •

"Stewart started a mission school in Upper Sandusky not FOR but WITH the Wyandott. . . . The Wyandott Indian Mission School of John Stewart and those who followed in his footsteps was a school run by blacks, whites, and Indians side by side. In this school, Native American culture and identity would not be shamed but be a key in coming together, established in the vision of a black man to have a school and a church together. . . . John Stewart's story gets at the heart of Christian mission. Words like acceptance, tolerance, collaboration, and breaking down barriers come to mind. Mission and ministry WITH instead of TO and FOR others come to mind and stand in stark contrast to words like arrival, assessment, exploitation, occupation, forced assimilation or alienation—all too common in the paradigm of the history of Christian mission."

—*Rev. Alfred T. Day, III, General Secretary, General Commission on Archives and History, "The Legacy of John Stewart and the Wyandot," Methodist Mission Bicentennial Website, https://methodistmission200.org/about-the-bicentennial/the-legacy-of-john-stewart-and-the-wyandot/*

• •

Part of the answer to this question was in how the bicentennial presented the story of Methodist mission history. Planners tried to ensure that the stories we lifted up—in the story collection, at the conference, and in presentations to other groups—represented not only white American men, but the full range of people who have been part of Methodist mission, past and present. This is why the story of John Stewart and the Wyandot is such an important one—it is a reminder that Global Ministries had its origins not in some top-down denominational scheme, but in a faithful act of mission from the margins. During the conference, participants honored the memory of John Stewart. The return of land in Upper Sandusky, held in trust by Global Ministries since 1843, to the Wyandotte Nation was also such an important part of the bicentennial because it recognized this important dimension of what history says about the ability of people from all backgrounds to be part of God's story of mission.

••

Participating United Methodist and ecumenical church partners at the bicentennial conference:

The United Methodist Church representatives from Angola, Democratic Republic of Congo, Estonia, Germany, Liberia, Lithuania, Mozambique, Nigeria, Norway, Philippines, Russia, Senegal, Sierra Leone, United States of America, Zambia, Zimbabwe

La Iglesia Evangelica Metodista Argentina

A Igreja Metodista em Brasil

Methodist Church in Britain

The Methodist Church of the Caribbean and the Americas

United Church of Canada

China Christian Council

Methodist Church in Fiji and Rotuma

Free Methodist Church

The Methodist Church in Ghana

Methodist Church in India

Methodist Church Indonesia

United Church of Christ in Japan

Methodist Church in Kenya

Korean Methodist Church

La Iglesia Metodista de Mexico

La Iglesia Metodista de Puerto Rico

Methodist Church in Singapore

Methodist Church of Southern Africa

Methodist Church in Sri Lanka

• •

That intention to capture the breadth of those involved in God's mission was also reflected in who was represented on the steering committee and at the bicentennial conference. The steering committee included members from all global regions of The United Methodist Church. The conference attracted over 250 participants, including United Methodists from sixteen countries and representatives from at least twenty-one other Methodist-related communions. Participants, who represented thirty-five countries in all, included current and former missionaries, mission partners, mission volunteers, deans and professors, students, laity, clergy, bishops, and staff from general agencies. Not one of the four keynote speakers at the conference was a white American male, and three of the four of them were born outside the United States. Conference worship included music, prayers, and liturgy from a variety of cultural backgrounds, and those leading the worship included women and men from a range of racial, ethnic, and national identities. More information about the conference program and attendees is available in the appendices.

• •

"The event was very inspiring. I especially appreciated that representatives of autonomous Methodist churches attended, to honor our shared heritage. Our bicentennial celebration was much bigger than [The United Methodist Church], as it was meaningful for Methodist churches around the world. The presentation of stories from around the world underscored why shared celebration was key to the success of the event. . . . I especially appreciated seeing present and former mission leaders of all ages and nationalities. And of course, joint worship and shared meals embodied who we are . . . across the globe. Given the strains on the world communion, it was a real blessing to be united in celebration of our common mission heritage. It strengthened the essentials of our identity as followers of Jesus Christ."

—Dr. Dana L. Robert, bicentennial steering committee member, reflecting back on the bicentennial conference

• •

Past, Present, and Future

Bicentennial conference participants partake in a reaffirmation of baptism service.
Photo: Jennifer Silver, Global Ministries

"[Jesus] called his disciples to share in the baptism of his death and resurrection and then sent them out in mission to make disciples of all nations, baptizing in the name of the Father, Son, and Holy Spirit. Thus, through baptism we are incorporated into the ongoing history of your mission[, O God]. Through baptism, you call and commission us to the ministry of all Christian believers, a ministry grounded upon the awareness that we have been called by you into a new relationship not only with you, but also with the world. You call us to embody the gospel and the church in the world. You call us to exercise our calling by prayer, by witnessing to your good news of salvation in Christ, by caring for and serving other people, and by working toward reconciliation, justice, and peace in the world. This is our calling in mission by you as part of the universal priesthood of all believers, and we thank you for it."

—From the Missional Reaffirmation of Baptism liturgy used at the Methodist Mission Bicentennial Conference, Atlanta, April 2019

One last consideration went into the bicentennial planning. Throughout, bicentennial planners saw the bicentennial as about past, present, *and* future. Global Ministries emphasized that a key purpose for the bicentennial celebration was not only to reflect the diversity of mission undertaken by Methodists over the last 200 years, but also to honor mission in the current life of the church, to draw today's church further into God's mission, and to enable the church to reflect collectively on the calling of Methodist mission for the sake of moving forward. The collecting of mission stories and the bicentennial conference helped promote key questions facing mission and The United Methodist Church. What has the church learned from our past in mission? How is God moving among Methodists today? Where is God calling Methodists to go in mission in the future?

Global Ministries' bicentennial matters because it is not just about the past. It is about reaffirming who we as Methodists in mission have been and letting that past inform who we are becoming. Remembering our mission past inspires us to recommit today for the sake of our mission future. This goal characterizes this book as well: we the editors (David Scott and Thomas Kemper) hope you will take away from this book not just some interesting facts about the past. Instead, we hope it will leave you with a renewed desire to hear and answer God's call on you to mission, now and in the years to come.

Recommended Readings

For more on the principles of partnership and collaboration among partners, see:

- Glory E. Dharmaraj and Jacob S. Dharmaraj. *A Theology of Mutuality: A Paradigm for Mission in the Twenty-First Century.* New York: United Methodist Women, 2014.

- Amy Valdez Barker, ed. *Mission Roundtable: Trusting the Circle, Engaging with Dialogue.* Atlanta: Global Ministries, 2019. https://drive.google.com/file/d/14oByhjbAnfuBisRz9Toxcr5Ew jNYkEzF/view.

For more on the 1919 Mission Centenary, including its triumphalist tone, see:

- Christopher J. Anderson, *The Centenary Celebration of American Methodist Missions: The 1919 World's Fair of Evangelical Americanism.* Lewiston, NY: Edwin Mellen, 2012.

- Christopher J. Anderson, *Voices from the Fair: Race, Gender, and the American Nation at a Methodist Missionary Exposition.* Lexington, KY: Emeth, 2012.

- David W. Scott, "Commemorating Mission: History as a Means to Revival of the Missionary Spirit." Thirteenth Oxford Institute of Methodist Theological Studies, August 12–19, 2018. https://oimts.files.wordpress.com/2018/11/2018-06 -scott.pdf.

For collections of papers based on presentations at "Answering the Call," the Methodist Mission Bicentennial Conference, see:

- David W. Scott, guest ed. "Papers from the Methodist Mission Bicentennial Conference April 8–10, 2019." *Methodist History* 58, nos. 1–2 (October 2019 & January 2020).

- David W. Scott and Darryl W. Stephens, eds. *The Practice of Mission in Global Methodism: Emerging Trends from Everywhere to Everywhere.* New York: Routledge, forthcoming in 2021.

For the stories collected as part of the bicentennial celebration, see:

- "Mission Stories." Methodist Mission Bicentennial website. https://methodistmission200.org/mission-stories/.

- "History of Missiology." Boston University School of Theology. http://www.bu.edu/missiology/category/methodist-mission -bicentennial/.

For a video about the bicentennial shared with annual conferences and other audiences, see:

- "Methodist Mission Bicentennial Video." Global Ministries. YouTube. https://www.youtube.com/watch?v=8hrH_3KYCWc.

CHAPTER 2

THE VIRTUES
OF MISSION

Arun W. Jones

Christian mission can be a highly charged phrase, both within and outside the church. *History of Christian mission* can be even more highly charged. For some persons, mission represents the best of what our faith has offered to the world. For others, mission is the cause of great violence and ills that have been inflicted on the world in the last two thousand years. This last attitude was recently verbalized by a student of mine, who, when I started talking about Christian mission, immediately brought up, with deep pain and anger in his voice, the genocide of native peoples in the American continents. Of course, the history and current practice of Christian mission is far more complicated and complex than simple praise or condemnation would convey. And it is this complexity that makes it difficult for anyone to understand mission fully—which is probably why we tend to use quick and easy labels, loaded with our prejudices, to describe it.

Certain contexts can push us to look at Christian mission in a more positive or negative light. A seminary classroom is one such context; an anniversary celebration is quite another. This essay was originally written and delivered as a keynote address at a celebration of the bicentennial of American Methodist missions. The general assignment I had been given by the planning committee was to speak on the topic "The Voice of God in Missions Past." Needless to say, occasions like a bicentennial tend to encourage speakers to extol the movement being commemorated. And that is not inappropriate.

However, as a scholar, I wanted to highlight the positive aspects of Methodist mission in a responsible manner—in a way that did not completely ignore the harm that it has caused in the world (not that there is any human movement that has not caused some harm in the world). As you will see, that acknowledgment comes toward the beginning of the address. But the address itself is an attempt to draw out something of abiding value from mission work of the past in order to help us in our mission and church work today—including, as you will read at the end of the address, that work which is deeply problematic in The United Methodist Church.

I wrote this speech after having just finished a book on American Methodist and Presbyterian missions in North India in the nineteenth century. The material in that volume was still fresh on my mind. And so, when I started to work on the keynote address, I reflected on what I had found to be admirable and valuable in the Indian and foreign mission workers of the past. What of their lives could I convey to my fellow Methodists today? I realized that one trait of "successful" mission workers, whether native or foreign, was that they could work productively with competing demands on their lives. In fact, I had written a whole chapter on how evangelical North Indian church leaders of the nineteenth century were adept at negotiating the push and pull of their local cultures, on the one hand, and the Western missionaries with whom (and for whom) they worked, on the other.[1] Moreover, I had noted the tension between zeal and compassion in the rhetoric of Western missions.[2] While I had not evaluated that tension in my book, I had come to the conclusion that this tension was a productive one. What other tensions, I wondered, could I name that had helped to produce good fruit for these missions? The three tensions that are identified and briefly developed in the bicentennial keynote address are what I would end up identifying as the virtues of (Methodist) mission.[3]

---

1.   Arun W. Jones, *Missionary Christianity and Local Religion: American Evangelicalism in North India, 1836–1870* (Waco, TX: Baylor University Press, 2017), chapter 4.

2.   Jones, *Missionary Christianity and Local Religion*, 106–8.

3.   While the three virtues are certainly not exclusively found in Methodist mission, they grow out of qualities that are hallmarks of the Methodist movement: the emphasis on a personal relationship with God; the emphasis on the affective dimension of religious experience; and the emphasis on pragmatism in religious praxis.

My task as a scholar then became to learn something of value—something of God—from actual practitioners of mission in the past and to convey this valuable information to actual practitioners of mission in the present. At best, I could interpret the past to the present in a way that was useful to the latter; I could mediate between past and present practitioners by choosing and arranging historical information in ways helpful to our contemporary world; I could set up a conversation between past and present that required dignity and humility from all and for all concerned.

This is what I attempted to do in the address that follows. In its own way, the speech is an exhortation not to let the negativity of the past and present stop us from faithfully engaging in mission: knowing that our best efforts will be open to criticism, but also they will contain elements of great worth, some of which we have inherited from the past.

Rev. Dr. Arun W. Jones delivers the keynote address of the opening banquet of "Answering the Call," the Methodist Mission Bicentennial Conference, Atlanta, Georgia, April 8, 2019. *Photo: Jennifer Silver, Global Ministries*

Introduction

It is indeed a great honor to be invited to give the opening lecture at this auspicious occasion, the celebration of the bicentennial of American Methodist missions. I wish to offer my profound thanks to the steering committee for this opportunity. I am keenly aware that it is late in the evening, that all of us are full from a delicious dinner, that many of us are tired from traveling, and that we have had a number of wonderful and necessary presentations and speeches already this evening. In short, my speech must be brief.

Let me begin with the obvious. We are celebrating the bicentennial of Methodist missions not because Methodists—or for that matter any other group of Christians—have a largely unblemished record of mission work. In fact, as we look back honestly at two centuries of missions, we can see failures as well as successes, transgressions as well as righteousness, cowardice as well as heroism, and too often a reliance on the gods of this world rather than the God revealed to us in Jesus Christ. I also wish to be clear that our forebears in mission, taken together, were not any worse than we are. I do not subscribe to the belief that we are, as a whole, morally superior to our predecessors. In fact, we are just as flawed as they were. If we can avoid any of their errors, it is because we can learn from them. And like them, we often do not see our own errors, and we shall need our descendants to clearly perceive how we have fallen short of the goodness and truth and beauty of God.[4] So as we gather for this time of remembrance, we acknowledge and confess that our collective work of mission, both in the past and continuing into the present, has indeed been at times deeply flawed, as we have claimed to work in Christ's name.

So, if we have not come here to praise Methodist missions, why are we here? We can respond with a famous line from Charles Wesley, "O for a thousand tongues to sing my great *Redeemer's* praise."[5] We have come together for these days of reflection and celebration to praise *God*, who has seen it fit to use our all too human nature for God's work; to remember with gratitude and joy those people and those events through whom God's will has indeed

---

4. See Andrew F. Walls, "The Ephesian Moment: At a Crossroads in Christian History," in *The Cross-Cultural Process in Christian History* (Maryknoll, NY: Orbis Books, 2002), 73.

5. Charles Wesley, "O For a Thousand Tongues to Sing," *The United Methodist Hymnal* (Nashville: The United Methodist Publishing House, 1989), 57 (italics added).

been done on earth as it is in heaven; and to commit ourselves once again to demonstrating to the world the incredibly vast love of God that we have come to know in Christ Jesus.

My assignment this evening is to draw our attention to the voice of God in Methodist missions in the past. In other words, *What is it that is truly of God that we can perceive in the history of Methodist missions over these past 200 years?* This question will have as many answers as there are people to answer it, as the hundreds of mission stories on the Methodist Mission Bicentennial webpage amply witness.[6] Please read some of them. God has been at work in uncountable lives and deeds of the people called Methodist, and one of the purposes of this bicentennial is to celebrate all the different ways we perceive Christ's presence and activity in the world through the ages, thanks to the work of Methodist missions.

This evening, however, I wish to identify certain virtues that I believe have been demonstrated in Methodist mission when it has been done rightly, when it has truly been the vehicle of God's voice in the world. There are three pairs of virtues that I would like to highlight. You will see that in each pair, the virtues are in tension with each other. They pull the missionary in different directions, they cause her to stop and take stock of the situations in which she finds herself, they complicate rather than simplify Christian mission, but they also show how rich and deep and complex is the voice of God as it is heard in Christian mission. The three pairs of virtues I would name are as follows: First, it is the ability to respond to the voice of God as it comes directly to us, but also to respond to the voice of God as it is spoken to us by the people around us. Second, it is to have a great zeal for our work, but also to have deep compassion for the people with whom we work. Third and finally, it is the determination to persevere through all sorts of adversities and difficulties, but also the openness and skill to adapt to new and unfolding situations. Responding to God's voice within and without; zeal and compassion; perseverance and adaptation: let me briefly illustrate these three sets of virtues from the life of John Stewart, the first missionary of the Methodist Episcopal Church, who went to the Wyandot people in Ohio.

---

6. "Methodist Mission Bicentennial," https://methodistmission200.org.

The Life of John Stewart

Photo: Jennifer Silver, Global Ministries

"On this night that launches the bicentennial of Methodist mission, bearing the gospel of Jesus Christ from everywhere to everywhere, we pause to return to the beginning of it all—an old story, a new story, a story that never gets old. . . . John Stewart attended a . . . Methodist camp and prayer meeting and entered into a period of deep reflection after a dark night in his own soul. . . . Here we are tonight, remembering our beginnings in mission . . . crossing boundaries that no one thought were humanly possible, doing great things in the name of Jesus Christ. . . . We celebrate the beginning of Methodist mission in America by welcoming Wyandotte brothers and sisters and remembering our beginnings in Methodist mission."

—*Rev. Alfred T. Day III, General Secretary, General Commission on Archives and History, at the Methodist Mission Bicentennial Conference, Atlanta, April 2019, opening banquet recognition of John Stewart and the Wyandotte*

Stewart has a very interesting biography. He was of mixed ancestry: he was a free-born "mulatto" with Native American heritage, although from which native people he did not know.[7] Moreover, we are told that "he became disabled early in life"—but again, we do not know his disability.[8] He was left behind in Virginia, where he was born in 1786, when his parents moved to Tennessee. It seems he had little, if any formal education; he is referred to as "unlettered" and "a man of no learning."[9] When he reached young adulthood, he set off to reunite with his parents, but on the way was robbed of everything he had. Penniless, he eventually ended up in Ohio, where his life quickly dissolved into one of alcoholic ruin, to the point where he could scarcely even feed himself, and he determined to commit suicide. Fortunately, the tavern keeper refused to give him any more alcohol, and so he regained his sobriety, and after many ups and downs, including a brief return to drink, he experienced a conversion and joined the Methodist Episcopal Church.

In the fall of 1814, he was stricken by a disease that he was sure was going to kill him. He prayed to God, promising that he would become a preacher if he survived. He then went into a field to pray. Here are his words of what he experienced there: "It seemed to me that I heard a voice, like the voice of a woman praising God; and then another, as a voice of a man, saying to me, 'You must declare my counsel faithfully.' These voices ran through me powerfully. They seemed to come from a northwest direction. . . . [It] seemed an indication to me that the Lord had called me to warn sinners to flee the wrath to come."[10] Soon after, John Stewart set out in a northwest direction to discover where the Lord was calling him to preach and minister, and eventually ended up in 1816 among the Wyandot people in Ohio. The spiritual and physical journey of John Stewart to the Wyandots was long and circuitous. I would, however, like to highlight three people crucial to his mission. The first two were a married couple, Mr. and Mrs. Walker. Mr. Walker was the federal agent dealing with the Wyandot. His wife was half Wyandot and well educated; "she possessed great influence in the nation" we are told, and it was her word that allowed the people to first accept John

---

7.   James B. Finley, *History of the Wyandott Mission, at Upper Sandusky, Ohio, under the Direction of the Methodist Episcopal Church* (Cincinnati: J. F. Wright and L. Swormstedt, 1840), 74; Stewart's biography is taken from 74–95.

8.   Finley, *History of the Wyandott Mission*, 74.

9.   Finley, *History of the Wyandott Mission*, 95, 74.

10.   Finley, *History of the Wyandott Mission*, 76.

Stewart.[11] She and her husband spoke the Wyandot language fluently. The third person was another African American, Jonathan Pointer, who had been taken prisoner as a boy by the Wyandot in what is now West Virginia, raised by them, and also spoke their language fluently. Jonathan Pointer was the reluctant interpreter for John Stewart, our Methodist missionary; Pointer didn't believe that the Wyandot wanted or needed another religion.[12] However, Stewart was committed to preaching to the Wyandot, so he accompanied Pointer to a Wyandot feast the next day, and asked Pointer to introduce him to the leaders as "a friend to their souls."[13] Thereafter Stewart started his evangelistic ministry to the people, with Pointer as his interpreter, by visiting them and telling them to "flee from the wrath that is to come," the classic Wesleyan message.[14] The response to his message was extremely disheartening: at first, only one or two elderly people showed up to hear him. Slowly, over the course of time, the number of visitors started to increase. Interestingly, what most fascinated the small group that came to hear Stewart was not his preaching but his singing. We are told that Stewart quickly learned to "mix his prayers and exhortations with songs."[15] Many of the Wyandot in fact had been Roman Catholics before, and as Stewart sang and prayed and preached, they started to remember their Catholic songs and prayers. That did not go over very well with the young Methodist evangelist! Eventually, Jonathan Pointer himself was converted.

The story of Stewart's ministry among the Wyandot is, as I have said, a fascinating one. His success was, at best, mixed and limited. A number of the most powerful leaders of the people—both women and men—opposed any change of religion, although others were open to Stewart's message and over time were converted. In fact, Stewart left the Wyandot for several months after a discouraging encounter with some powerful Wyandot chiefs, returning later to resume his ministry. His work was also opposed by rival evangelists. But Stewart, along with his wife, settled down and lived and ministered among the Wyandot, until his death in 1823.

---

11.   Finley, *History of the Wyandott Mission*, 78.

12.   Finley, *History of the Wyandott Mission*, 79.

13.   Finley, *History of the Wyandott Mission*, 79.

14.   Finley, *History of the Wyandott Mission*, 79.

15.   Finley, *History of the Wyandott Mission*, 80.

The Voice of God Within and Without

God of Mission, you have called your church
to witness in the world till the end of the age.
You have called the people called Methodists
to be vulnerably available at your service
and resiliently hopeful
amidst anxieties, fears, crises, and conflicts.
Call us afresh and lead us to mission.

—Methodist Mission Bicentennial Conference, Atlanta, April 2019,
opening banquet, from the opening prayer, written by the worship team

John Stewart's path-breaking ministry—although we must not forget the Roman Catholic missionaries who came before him—exemplifies the virtues of mission that I articulated earlier. First, he responded to the voice of God as it came to him: remember how he heard a woman's and a man's voice in an open field, coming from the northwest, telling him to declare God's counsels faithfully. And so he set out to the northwest, eventually arriving at the home of some of the Wyandot people. Yet Stewart also was attentive to God's voice as it came to him from others. Surprisingly, he took seriously the opinions of the Wyandot who opposed him on theological grounds. The first time that he urged the people to give up their ancestral religion and become Christians, he requested any who opposed his message to speak up. At that point one of the chiefs, John Hicks, stood up and said,

> My friend, . . . I feel called on to arise in defense of the religion of my fa-
> thers. The Great Spirit has given his red children a religion to guide their
> feet, and to establish them in the good way, and we do not feel like leaving
> it so soon as you wish us to do. We have been deceived several times by the
> Seneca and Shawnee prophets, and had to return to our old religion, and
> find it the best of any for us. We are contented with it; because it suits our
> conditions, and is adapted to our capacities. Cast your eyes over the world,
> and you will see that the Great Spirit has given to every nation a religion
> suited to their condition; and these all differ. Is this not the work of the
> Great Spirit? My friend, your speaking so violently against the modes of
> our worship is not calculated to do us much good. We are willing to receive
> good advice from you, but we are not willing to have the religion and cus-
> toms of our fathers thus assailed and abused.[16]

---

16.   Finley, *History of the Wyandott Mission*, 82.

That John Stewart took to heart the words of this chief, and others who thought like him, became evident in a letter that Stewart sent to the Wyandot several months later, while he was separated from them.[17] In this letter, he again makes an appeal to his Wyandot friends to follow the Christian way, but his letter reveals two new ways of thinking about his own religion. Quoting Matthew 5:6, "Happy are people who are hungry and thirsty for righteousness, because they will be fed until they are full," Stewart tells the Wyandot that the purpose of Christianity is to inculcate righteousness in the here and now—something that the chief and other Wyandot were also very concerned about. In fact, one of the big draws of Methodism for some of the Wyandot was its prohibition of alcohol, which was creating havoc and ruin among their people.[18] A second way in which Stewart heeded the voice of God as articulated by the Wyandot chief is that he took seriously God's self-revelation as Spirit. Stewart's letter to the Wyandot is, as we might expect, filled with references to Jesus Christ. However, what is interesting is how the letter is also filled with references to the Spirit of God, and how he admonishes the Wyandot not to grieve the Spirit by doing evil and rejecting the ways of good. Stewart's attention to the work of the Spirit later on allowed the first generation of Christian Wyandot to identify God the Father as well as the Holy Spirit with the Great Spirit—God's unique self-revelation to them and other First Nations through their ancestors.[19]

Zeal and Compassion

So good missionaries have paid attention to the voice of God as it comes to them, but also as it has been articulated by the people around them. A second pair of virtues exemplified by missionaries in the past is that they are pos-

---

17.   Finley, *History of the Wyandott Mission*, 87–92. The existence of a letter, which is also recorded in *The Missionary Pioneer, or A Brief Memoir of the Life, Labours, and Death of John Stewart (Man of Colour), Founder, under God, of the Mission among the Wyandotts at Upper Sandusky, Ohio* (New York: Joseph Mitchell, 1827), from "a man of no learning" is never explained. It seems, from other evidence, that Stewart must have had some education, whether formal or not. For example, he taught in the first school that the Methodists put up: Finley, *History of the Wyandott Mission*, 141. On the other hand, Stewart could also have used an amanuensis to write his letter.

18.   Finley, *History of the Wyandott Mission*, 98–100, 132.

19.   For example, see Finley, *History of the Wyandott Mission*, 146, 158, 288.

sessed by both zeal and compassion.[20] These two virtues live in some tension with each other. Zeal implies a strong, even fierce stance toward the world; zealots are those who cling to their cause with little thought to the consequences to themselves or others. Compassion, on the other hand, implies an approach full of love and tenderness to the people one serves. If one loses zeal for one's work, one is liable to lose the purpose of one's ministry. If one loses compassion for the people among whom one ministers, one can ride roughshod over other people's lives as one determines to fulfill his or her mission.

Photo: Jennifer Silver, Global Ministries

"What really mattered then and still matters today is how we love one another and help those who need our help in mission and in service as we make disciples of Jesus Christ for the transformation of the world. . . . John Stewart served in mission not for gain, fame, or pleasure, but to save souls from the bondage of darkness. The risks were many. He felt that the hand of God was over him. And when you take a stand for God, God will take care of you. . . . In the providence of God, John Stewart . . . carried the gospel of love, the gospel of peace."

—*James H. Salley, Associate Vice Chancellor, Africa University, and member, Black Methodists for Church Renewal Board of Directors, at the Methodist Mission Bicentennial Conference, Atlanta, April 2019, opening banquet recognition of John Stewart and the Wyandotte*

---

20.   See Jones, *Missionary Christianity and Local Religion*, 106–8.

In John Stewart's life, the contrast between zeal and compassion comes through in the reports we have of his preaching, on the one hand, and his treatment of the Wyandot, on the other. To those of us who have been trained to be culturally sensitive, Stewart's preaching comes across as harsh and even inconsiderate: his attitude to both native and Roman Catholic religion was full of severe condemnation. Yet in his relationships with people, he was a deeply sensitive and compassionate person. When people opposed him, he listened to them attentively; he ministered lovingly to friend and foe alike when they were facing difficulties. On more than one occasion, a number of Wyandot said that they wanted Stewart (and his companion Jonathan Pointer) to live among them as a representative of the Christian faith.[21] This difference between zealous words and compassionate deeds—both of which were important to John Stewart—are captured in Chief John Hicks's speech I quoted at length earlier.[22] The chief twice refers to Stewart as "friend," and says that the people are appreciative of the good advice that Stewart gives them. However, the chief criticizes his friend for speaking violently against Indian modes of worship. Some of this criticism, as I said, Stewart takes to heart; but he never ceases to be a zealous proclaimer of the gospel of Jesus Christ, as well as a compassionate man of God.

Perseverance and Adaptation

• •

"Two hundred years ago, [missionaries] went uncertain of the success of their mission, but totally convinced of the worthiness of their message. . . . They believed that their mission of spreading scriptural holiness, their mission of sharing their faith in Jesus Christ with those who were yet to know him, was much more valuable than their lives. . . . We gather here, not only to celebrate their sacrifice, commitment, and dedication, but in a very real sense, we gather here as fruits of their labor . . . blessed by their sacrifice and commitment and dedication. . . . My prayer is that . . . in 200 years, others will gather and say of us, we were faithful in answering the call, no matter what it cost us."

—Rev. Dr. Casely B. Essamuah, Secretary, Global Christian Forum, at the Methodist Mission Bicentennial Conference, Atlanta, April 2019, opening banquet recognition of John Stewart and the Wyandotte

• •

---

21. Finley, *History of the Wyandott Mission*, 85, 105, 107.

22. Finley, *History of the Wyandott Mission*, 82.

The final pair of virtues of mission that I would like to lift up is perseverance and adaptation. Perseverance entails pushing through difficulties and obstacles in order to reach our goal in life; adaptation involves changing our plans and ideas to suit new circumstances as they present themselves. Stewart's remarkable perseverance is demonstrated through his biography: once he reached the Wyandot in Ohio, he refused to give up his ministry, living to the very end among the people he served, despite much opposition from various quarters, despite the fact that every time he thought he had gathered a band of truly converted Wyandot, he would discover at a feast that many of them still appreciated the traditional religion of their own people.[23] Yet this perseverance was marked by constant adjustments and changes in Stewart's work as he carried out his mission. One of the early challenges to his ministry came from another group of missionaries—we are not told which denomination they belonged to—who also came to the Wyandot, and told the people that Stewart had no authority to work as a missionary; he had only been licensed as a Methodist exhorter. This was, in fact, the truth—and made Stewart seem like a fraud. So, Stewart set out to receive credentialing as a Methodist preacher. These credentials he received in March of 1819 at a quarterly conference in Urbana, Ohio, and was licensed as a preacher and appointed to work as a missionary with the Wyandot.[24] Thus it was because of his positive, adaptive response to hostile challenges that John Stewart became the first Methodist missionary to the Wyandot. John Stewart was one who persevered in mission to the end of his life, while adapting his thought and work to deal with circumstances as they arose.

Closing Observations

I have used the life of John Stewart to illustrate what I have come to see as the virtues of Methodist missionaries more generally in ages past. These missionaries were women and men; some of them were young adults. They came from different races, and from all walks of life, all segments of society. They paid heed to the voice of God within them and to the voice of God speaking to them through others. They possessed both zeal and compassion in their

---

23. Finley, *History of the Wyandott Mission*, 79–85, 92–95.

24. Finley, *History of the Wyandott Mission*, 93–95.

work. And they exhibited great perseverance in their task, as well as great skill in adapting to differing circumstances.

I would like to close with two observations. The first is that while these three pairs of virtues are not uniquely Wesleyan, I would say they are quint-essentially Wesleyan. Methodism was launched in the eighteenth century as a movement to reform both individuals and society at large. The movement paid careful attention to the affective dimension of human life—to human emotions and feelings, as John Wesley's strangely warmed heart attests. Meth-odists also paid close attention and responded to their local conditions and contexts. This combination of desire for personal and social reform, of valu-ing the life of the heart, and of learning from experience, is what gave rise to the virtues I have highlighted from Methodist missions in the past.

My last observation has to do with how that past may speak to us today. We all know that our church, our denomination, is facing a particularly dif-ficult period at this time. We are living through an era of deep divisions and discord. We are split into various parties that are pitted against one another. At the risk of oversimplifying, it seems to me that we pay attention to what God is saying to us personally, without taking seriously enough what God is saying to us through others, especially those who may oppose us. We are full of zeal but wanting in compassion. We believe in perseverance but avoid adaptation. The voice of God from missions past calls us to learn from the virtues of our forebears, women and men who spread the good news of Jesus Christ all over the world. Could it be that our church today needs to heed the witness of missionaries such as John Stewart: a poor, "unlettered" black man, who nonetheless proclaimed the gospel to a people he did not know, for a future he could never imagine?

Recommended Readings

Two biographies of John Stewart, one written shortly after his death and the other written by a later pastor of the Methodist church in Upper San-dusky are available electronically:

- N. B. C. Love. *John Stewart: Missionary to the Wyandots.* New York: The Missionary Society of the Methodist Episcopal Church, 1900. https://archive.org/details/johnstewart missi00love/page/n1/mode/2up.

- Joseph Mitchell. *The Missionary Pioneer, or, a Brief Memoir of the Life, Labours, and Death of John Stewart (Man of Color), Founder, under God, of the Mission among the Wyandotts at Upper Sandusky, Ohio.* New York: J. C. Totten, 1827. https:// archive.org/details/missionarypionee00mitc.

As Arun Jones demonstrates with John Stewart, biographies of notable Methodist missionaries can be a good way to see some of the "virtues of mission" in action. Here are some additional recent biographies of Methodist missionaries:

- Pamela D. Couture. *We Are Not All Victims: Local Peacebuilding in the Democratic Republic of Congo.* Zurich: LIT, 2016. Bishop Ntambo Nkulu Ntanda pursued a holistic vision of mission and peacebuilding in the North Katanga Episcopal Area of The United Methodist Church during the First and Second Congo Wars.

- S. T. Kimbrough. *Sister Anna Eklund, 1867–1949: A Methodist Saint in Russia; Her Words and Witness, St. Petersburg 1908–1931.* New York: General Board of Global Ministries, The United Methodist Church, 2001. Eklund was a deaconess from Finland and one of the founders of Russian Methodism, serving the poor there.

- Jared Maddox. *Nathan Bangs and the Methodist Episcopal Church: The Spread of Scriptural Holiness in Nineteenth-Century America.* Nashville: New Room Books, 2018. Nathan Bangs helped found the Missionary Society of the Methodist Episcopal Church.

- Kristen Kobes du Mez. *A New Gospel for Women: Katharine Bushnell and the Challenge of Christian Feminism.* New York: Oxford University Press, 2015. Bushnell was a medical missionary in China and social reformer on behalf of women's issues in the United States and throughout the world.

- Robert G. Tuttle Jr. *In Our Time: The Life and Ministry of E. Stanley Jones.* Potomac, MD: E. Stanley Jones Foundation,

2019. E. Stanley Jones was one of the most famous Methodist missionaries, working in India in interreligious dialogue, peace-building, and other areas.

- Douglas D. Tzan. *William Taylor and the Mapping of the Methodist Missionary Tradition: The World His Parish*. Lanham, MD: Lexington Books, 2019. Taylor was a wide-ranging global evangelist and missionary bishop for the Methodist Episcopal Church who helped establish Methodism in parts of South American and Angola.

CHAPTER 3

LESSONS FROM 200 YEARS OF MISSION HISTORY

David W. Scott

O ver two centuries have passed since John Stewart arrived among the Wyandot and since news of his work inspired Nathan Bangs and other Methodist leaders in New York City to form the Missionary Society of the Methodist Episcopal Church. Over those two centuries, that organization has endured through many name changes, mergers, and reorganizations. Global Ministries stands as the present-day successor to the Missionary Society (and numerous other denominational mission organizations—see appendix A). Accordingly, it celebrated its 200th anniversary in 2019.

As the church has been commemorating that important milestone, Global Ministries has been reflecting upon what it has learned about mission by looking back over stories from this mission past. In the previous chapter, Arun Jones highlighted three pairs of recurring virtues that he has identified in that span of Methodist mission history, as exemplified by John Stewart: responding to the voice of God as heard individually and through others; balancing great zeal for our work with deep compassion for the people with whom we work; and perseverance through difficulties combined with adapting to new situations.

What follows are some additional lessons that Global Ministries as an organization has taken from its history. In some way, each of these lessons touches upon the combination of the human and the divine within mission: the tension between human structure and divine initiative; the impact of human systems of oppression such as racism, sexism, and colonialism on God's mission; the breadth of human activities encompassed within the scope of God's redemptive work; and enduring faithfulness to God's divine grace through the trials, tribulations, successes, and failures of our human efforts.

Mission, Structure, and Movement

. . . .

"United Methodists are by nature active and activist in our spirituality. We open our hands and share what we have received. But in this moment The United Methodist Church also extends her collective arms to the triune God. Whether we know it or not, we are the recipients of God's mission. . . . On behalf of the Council of Bishops of The United Methodist Church, each of whom has made a promise to unify the church and to support the mission, I celebrate this bicentennial of Methodist mission. Our predecessor bodies signify the ways we have not been faithful, or united, or fruitful. And yet through it all, there has been a treasure in this earthen vessel."

—*Bishop Ken Carter, President, Council of Bishops, The United Methodist Church, at the Methodist Mission Bicentennial Conference, Atlanta, April 2019, opening banquet*

. . . .

One of the most important insights that Global Ministries has learned about mission in the past two centuries is that mission is the *missio Dei* (mission of God), not the *missio ecclesia* (mission of the church). That means that mission is primarily about God and God's activity. As Global Ministries' Theology of Mission statement says, mission "begins with God, belongs to God, and will be fulfilled by God at the end of time."[1] Humans have an important role within mission—God carries out mission in, through, and with people—but God is the ultimate actor in, ground for, and focus of Christian mission. The following chapter, "Mission Concepts and Relationships, 2010–2020," expands upon this point further and demonstrates how a theology of *missio Dei* has shaped the work of Global Ministries over the past decade.

If mission is primarily about God, then it is not primarily about church structures or denominational organizations. Indeed, as noted above, these have changed many times over the past 200 years, even though there is also

---

1. See appendix B, or "Our Theology of Mission," Global Ministries, https://umcmission .org/our-theology-of-mission/.

continuity in the midst of these changes. But as Nathan Bangs and the others who organized the Missionary Society of the Methodist Episcopal Church recognized in their justification for doing so, organization matters. Formal mission structures allow the church to do more than it otherwise would be able to. Thus, throughout Methodist mission history, mission theologically understood as the *missio Dei* has stood in tension with mission as humanly shaped into organizations. This tension between divine initiative and human organization is one of the primary tensions amid which United Methodists and their predecessors have served.

John and Helen Springer, Mr. Heinkel (a teacher), and the boys. Fox Bible School, Kalulua, Congo, 1911.
Photo: GCAH Mission Photograph Album - Africa #1 page 0059

"Although Methodist missionaries ventured into the Belgian Congo before John Springer, his enterprising evangelistic explorations are credited with the founding of the present-day United Methodist Church in the Democratic Republic of the Congo. In 1901, Springer set sail for Africa. All that was left of Bishop William Taylor's work in the Congo and Zambia were two mission stations. In 1906, Springer and, by then, his wife, Helen Emily Chapman Rasmussen reached the Belgian Congo. Springer sparred with his New York mission secretary, Adna Leonard, who declared that divine inspiration was not a good excuse for John to ignore his bishop,

Joseph C. Hartzell, and strike out on his own. Springer continued to be a somewhat controversial figure. From 1921, his own missionaries in the Congo were upset with one of his impromptu acquisition attempts—Mulungwishi, which he finally acquired in 1937, with plans to build a Congo Institute, later named the Springer Institute. In 1936, John Springer was elected to serve as bishop for the Africa missions. Under his watch, the missions of the southern Congo and the missions of the northern Congo, established by southern Methodists in Wembo Nyama in the 1920s under Bishop Walter Lambuth, were brought together under one united church."

—Adapted from Christie R. House, "Springer, Bishop John McKendree (1873-1963)," Methodist Mission Bicentennial Website, https://methodist mission200.org/springer-bishop-john-mckendree-1873-1963/

• •

At times, this tension has led individual missionaries to insist that they had a privileged understanding of how God was acting in the world. Often, such missionaries insisted that they were following God's will, and the mission agency was standing as an impediment to what God really wanted done. One thinks of William Taylor's up and down relationship with the Missionary Society, or of John and Helen Springer's insistence on beginning work in what is now the Democratic Republic of Congo (DRC), despite the objections of the mission board. Here is perhaps an overlap between the tension between divine initiative and human structure and the tension Arun Jones identified between hearing the call of God individually and through others.

Looking back with the benefit of historical perspective, it is easier to see that personal egos and ambitions, not just different understandings of divine calling, were part of such conflicts. Nevertheless, one can also see how God worked through figures such as Taylor and the Springers to build the church in places like Angola and the DRC despite opposition from formal church structures. The work the Springers began in collaboration with indigenous evangelists like Tshangand Kayeke has now become the largest episcopal area in The United Methodist Church—the North Katanga area, which has over a million members. Is this not God's doing?

As Global Ministries today tries to live into this insight about the tension between divine movement and human structure, it encourages missionaries to focus not so much on insisting upon their own understanding of who God is and what God is doing, but rather to look beyond formal structures to see what God is doing in the communities where they serve. As Global Ministries' Theology of Mission statement says, "Partners in God's mission seek to hear God's voice, to discover the signs of the moving of the Spirit through the world today, and to bear witness to God's activity—overarching past, pres-

34

ent, and future—in every local setting." To respond to divine initiative means to be always curious, always learning, and always ready to adapt and change when we encounter God in surprising ways.

This willingness to change is another way in which Global Ministries has experienced the distinction and connection between human structure and divine leading. A list of changes in organizational policy, structure, positions, and procedures that have characterized the past 200 years of Global Ministries' existence would certainly run to many pages. Some of these have reflected changes outside the agency itself, as when denominational mergers in 1939 (Methodist Episcopal Church, Methodist Episcopal Church, South, and Methodist Protestant Church), 1946 (Evangelical Church and United Brethren in Christ), and 1968 (The Methodist Church and Evangelical United Brethren Church) also led to mergers of the missionary societies associated with those denominations.

Yet often the reorganizations that happened at Global Ministries and its predecessors reflected an attempt to be more faithful to God's call in mission, as people came to understand how God was leading them in new ways in new situations. Thus, the 1996 restructure, which eliminated the previous World Division and National Division, was an attempt to better live into an understanding that God's mission is one mission throughout the world. The formation of the United Methodist Missionary Association was connected to an attempt by agency leaders to better listen to what God was saying through the missionaries of the agency. The regional restructuring in 2016 was an attempt to embody what God had taught the agency about the importance of relationships with people living and working in the various contexts of ministry where Global Ministries works. In all of these efforts and others, leaders at Global Ministries recognized that what was most important was faithfulness to God's calling to participate in the *missio Dei*, not faithfulness to a particular organizational structure.

This insight means that in its work now, Global Ministries continues to innovate and change its structures for the sake of better responding to how it discerns God's calling to participate in the *missio Dei*, and one may expect it to continue to do so. Change is healthy and a sign of commitment to mission, not particular structures. Moreover, there will continue to be changes within Global Ministries and within The United Methodist Church as a denomination. Yet whatever changes occur, they will not prevent faithful Methodists from continuing to participate in the *missio Dei*. Structures may change, but

God will remain the same. As Christians, we do not need to fear change but instead should be ready to discover how, through change, we can continue to be faithful to God's calling in new times and new contexts.

Power, Oppression, and Mission from the Margins

••

"Good evening, friends. . . . This 200th anniversary, like United Methodist Women's 150th . . . is an opportunity . . . to give thanks for the many who have served, the lives that have been touched, and the growth of churches and of movements. We give thanks for all who have participated in the sending and the support . . . and for all who supported . . . this movement from Missionary Society to General Board of Global Ministries. We also reflect on some of the failings and the errors of the past. When Thomas was with us in Boston to celebrate our 150th last month, he shared an important acknowledgement of the way patriarchy has affected the women's mission work over this long period of time. It was a powerful moment. . . . I want to say [again] thank you. . . . We might both make similar acknowledgements of the role that colonialism and racism and other '-isms' have played in affecting both our efforts and causing harm where we intended good. In this era, both of our organizations are working to see this clearly enough to establish different relationships with mission partners—autonomous churches, institutions, and movements around the world—[and] to approach the future in new ways."

—*Harriett Olson, General Secretary, United Methodist Women, at the Methodist Mission Bicentennial Conference, Atlanta, April 2019, opening banquet*

••

While mission should not be identified with structures, structure and organization have been very important in this history of Methodist mission. Yet they are a double-edged sword. On the positive side, such structures and organizations are a main means through which humans respond to God's calling to mission. They allow Methodists to cooperate in the spirit of connectionalism. They mobilize people and money in significant ways. They connect Methodists around the world. God and humans working together through human structures have been able to accomplish amazing things. People have come to know Jesus. They have learned to read, write, and practice new skills. They have been healed in body and mind. Peace has been made between enemies. Justice has been championed. Missionaries, mission agencies, and indigenous mission leaders have been important players in promoting civil rights in the

United States and self-determination for people around the globe. None of these fruits of God's mission should be disparaged, and the role of human structures in supporting these accomplishments must be acknowledged.

Yet, on the negative side, these structures have also sometimes been structures of oppression that have hurt and excluded people based on race, gender, nationality, class, ability, and other dimensions of difference. Human sinfulness affects not just individuals, but communities and organizations as well. So it has been in the history of Methodist mission. Thus, individual Methodists have expressed personal prejudice or acted in hurtful and hateful ways toward those who were different from them. But our connectional structures have also at times systematized the prejudices of their members.

••

"I think it is fair to say that Methodist history includes and reflects the good and bad of its times. Paternalism and Western superiority can be found there but so can mutual admiration, respect, and deep compassion among missionaries and the people they served. There is evidence of prejudice concerning race and gender but also of trial and error, learning and acceptance. Throughout [and] in all places, dedicated and faithful people accepted the love of Christ the missionaries offered and became part of their own mission history."

—*Christie House, editor,* New World Outlook, *"200 Years of Mission History,"* New World Outlook, *Fall 2018*

••

There are many such examples, but it is worth naming a few specific ones here. Plantation missions were based on a racist belief that it was possible to care about the status of the souls of enslaved African Americans without seeing them as full humans, equal with white Americans and equally deserving of freedom. When The Methodist Church was created in 1939 with a racially segregated Central Jurisdiction, that segregation extended to its mission structures. Mission-run schools for Native Americans reflected a false belief among many white Methodists that God could not speak to Native Americans through their own languages and cultural histories, which white Americans believed needed to be destroyed. From the foundation of the Women's Foreign Missionary Society of the Methodist Episcopal Church in 1869, culminating in the 1964 restructuring of The Methodist Church's Board of Mission, women's organizations were repeatedly made subservient to male-controlled denominational agencies, and men were happy to take the money women raised without according them a say in how that money was used. Throughout the world, native evangelists and pastors found that they were not seen or treated as equal to Western missionaries, and both native leaders and missionaries often felt as if the needs and perspectives of the mission board in New York were prioritized over the needs and perspectives of local mission contexts. While Methodists need to celebrate the good that has been accomplished in our mission history, we also need to lament and repent of the harm that has been done in our mission history.

Yet within that repentance, hear this word of affirmation. The Greek word for repentance is *metanoia*, which means "turning away from." Turning away from prejudiced forms of thinking that elevate the experiences of white American males over those of all others allows one to see that mission has always originated not just from the center, but even more significantly from the margins and from marginalized people. Certainly, white American men have accomplished some great things for God in mission. But so too have people of color in the United States, indigenous leaders around the world, women, and the poor. Despite their lack of privilege in worldly ways, God has called such individuals to serve God in mission, and they have responded in faithfulness, whether or not that has always been acknowledged by those in the seats of power. Moreover, the margins are usually where revival, new initiatives for mission, and new ways of thinking about mission have come from.

While those at the center may just now be recognizing the value of "mission from the margins" and "mission from everywhere to everywhere," these are not new phenomena. Even though these phrases may be new, they reflect old experiences. African Americans and Native Americans have been serving in Methodist mission at least since John Stewart and the Wyandot. (And before if one regards as missionaries the evangelists such as Black Harry Hosier, one of the preeminent preachers and evangelists of Methodism in the British Colonies.) Methodists in the United States would not have existed without the missionary efforts of Barbara Heck, and there were women serving as missionaries for the Missionary Society starting with Ann Wilkins in 1837.

● ●

"Ann Wilkins was a missionary to Liberia from 1837–1857. She was the first American Methodist female missionary sent out by the Missionary Society of the Methodist Episcopal Church as a missionary herself and not as a missionary spouse. Wilkins first offered to go as a teacher to Liberia in 1834, but the Missionary Society took no action on her application at the time. Then, two years later, she attended a Methodist camp meeting in Sing Sing, NY. She sent a note to Nathan Bangs of the Missionary Society declaring, 'A sister who has but little money at command, gives that little cheerfully, and is willing to give her life as a female teacher, if she is wanted.' This time, Wilkins' application was accepted. After teaching in the White Plains Manual Labor School and at the Liberia Conference Seminary (now the College of West Africa), Wilkins founded the Millsburg Female Academy, which would be the focus of her ministry for the remainder of her time in

Liberia. In addition to its innovative work in girls' education, the seminary was notable as one of the first mission institutions dedicated to serving indigenous Liberians and not just Americo-Liberian settlers."

—*Adapted from David W. Scott, "Wilkins, Ann (1806–1857)," Methodist Mission Bicentennial Website, https://methodistmission200.org/ann-wilkins-1806-1857/*

Image: from The Ladies' Repository, 1859.

. . . .

Over the past two centuries, people from outside the United States, including Germans, Swedes, Danes, Norwegians, Irish, Britons, Canadians, and Australians all served as formal missionaries for the predecessors of Global Ministries, and people of a whole host of nationalities and ethnicities served as pastors, evangelists, teachers, and Bible women and colporteurs (who distributed Bibles and taught people to read them), usually but not always in their own home contexts. Francisco Penzotti, the founder of Methodism in several South American countries, served as a colporteur. Especially over the past half century, Global Ministries itself has benefited from staff leadership by women of all races and nationalities, people of color from the United States, and citizens of countries around the world.

Francisco Penzotti
Photo: GCAH Mission Photograph
Album - South America #2 page 0081

"Francisco (also known as Francis) Penzotti, an Italian immigrant to Uruguay, encountered American Methodist missionaries in Montevideo. His first assignment after his conversion was with the Waldensian Church in Uruguay—a Protestant denomination from Italy, closely related to Methodists in Europe. He helped to establish mission churches across Uruguay at a time when the Roman Catholic Church held a viselike grip over most of Latin America. In 1883, the Methodist Episcopal Church sent Penzotti across the continent to Bolivia. He visited Venezuela, Panama, Colombia, Ecuador, Peru, and Chile. He established a church in Callao, the seaport of Lima, Peru. 'As soon as I arrived here I sought to bring the people together. . . . The attendance and interest have constantly increased.' This drew the attention of both the Catholic clergy and the Peruvian government, which had Penzotti arrested. After the Callao Methodist Society was formally organized, persecution intensified. Penzotti was again arrested. A couple of New York reporters published an article that garnered international interest. As a result, Penzotti was released after eight months of imprisonment. This international attention eased the persecution suffered by the church in Peru. In 1970, the Iglesia Metodista del Perú (IMP) became autonomous."

—Adapted from Christie R. House, "Penzotti, Francisco," Methodist Mission Bicentennial Website, https://methodistmission200.org/penzotti-francisco/

These missionaries and mission leaders from marginalized backgrounds were not unaware of the ways in which prejudice affected the church and its mission structures. Many of them experienced the church and its mission agencies as US-centric, racist, and sexist. Most were aware, at least on some level, of critiques of mission as connected to Western imperialism. Nevertheless, they also understood that God had important work for them to do for and through God's church, and they were determined to do that work despite the obstacles of human inequalities. In the process, they were able to transform not only communities around the world but the very structures that sought to limit their full participation in God's mission. Thus, it is simultaneously true that mission structures and activities have historically been tied to Western imperialism, sexism, and racism and at the same time true that these very structures have been a genuine means for the initiative and self-determination of those on the margins.

Global Ministries is still trying to act upon these insights into the importance of recognizing mission as flowing from everywhere to everywhere and the importance of affirming mission from the margins. Global Ministries' Theology of Mission statement says, "In response to God's call and the leading of the Holy Spirit, women and men, young and old, of all nations, stations, and races, and in all times and places, unite as the living body of Christ to join God's mission of redemption, bearing witness to God's presence in the world." The following chapter will expand upon current initiatives in this regard, such as an everywhere to everywhere model of missionaries; an emphasis on collaboration with and facilitation of, not domination over, mission partners around the world; and the process of wrestling with the question of how to stand in solidarity with those on the margins, especially indigenous people, young people, immigrants, and the materially poor.

God calls Christians individually and as a church to repent and turn away from forms of systemic oppression, and Global Ministries takes seriously its calling in this regard, despite a past of both successes and failures in this arena. Fortunately, the *missio Dei* goes beyond the successes and failures of any church structure. God's mission is a mission of justice and loving-kindness, no matter how well or how poorly humans respond.

The Breadth of Mission

Mission has not only been carried out by people from many different walks of life, it has involved many different forms of human activity. The *missio Dei* incorporates the whole breadth of God's redemptive work in the world, or what Global Ministries' Theology of Mission statement refers to as "personal salvation, and social and cosmic transformation." Thus, since its beginnings, Methodist mission has combined evangelism, discipleship, education, health and healing, work with women and children, justice seeking, peacemaking, poverty relief and economic development, and agriculture. Moreover, over the course of 200 years of Methodist mission work, new areas of mission concern have emerged: work with immigrants and refugees, disaster relief, cross-cultural understanding, creation care, and others. Yet while there are different forms of mission, they all flow from the same theological understanding, as will be discussed in the chapter on mission and diakonia (or service). These various activities are all part of God's overall vision of redemption for the world God created and loves. Global Ministries understands mission holistically.

••

Ulysses S. Gray, missionary superintendent,
Gbarnga Mission, Liberia, 1950s
Photo: GCAH Mission Photograph Album - Africa #16, P. 72

Vivienne Gray teaching at the Harriet Tubman School,
Gbarnga Mission, Liberia
*Photo: GCAH Mission Photograph Album - Africa #16,
P. 75*

"The Rev. Ulysses Samuel Gray served as a missionary with the Methodist Board of Missions at the Gbarnga Mission Station in Bong County, Liberia, for nearly 27 years (1948–1974). His wife, Vivienne Newton Gray, also served the station as a teacher and administrator. Ulysses, known as 'U. S.,' served as mission superintendent, pastor for the Gbarnga church, and agricultural advisor for the mission station. He and Vivienne, one of a few African American couples assigned as international missionaries by the Board of Missions of the Methodist Church in the 1940s, oversaw the building and management of the church, homes, school, and the first gymnasium in the region. In 1959, U. S. Gray built the Gbarnga School of Theology. Ulysses and Vivienne Gray were honored with the Liberian Star by the Liberian government for their nearly 27 years in mission in Gbarnga. The Liberian Star medal is the highest honor that can be awarded to a civilian in the country."

—*Adapted from Christie R. House, "Gray, Ulysses Samuel (1913–2009)," Methodist Mission Bicentennial Website, https://methodistmission200.org/gray-ulysses-samuel-1913-2009/*

••

This holistic understanding of mission continues to shape the work of Global Ministries today. Global Ministries continues to engage in a variety of different forms of mission. In particular, Global Ministries is focused on building relationships and capacities among global mission partners to help facilitate how they establish, lead, and grow the church in their regions; emphasizing the importance of global missionaries, young adult and other missionaries, and mission volunteers; promoting abundant health for all, especially children, with special attention to the economically vulnerable; and increasing humanitarian assistance more fully and regularly by integrating immediate disaster response with long-term sustainable development. You will read more about these various forms of mission work and their theological underpinnings in the following two chapters.

Enduring Faithfulness

••

"In 1891, the Women's Missionary Association of the United Brethren in Christ sent Dr. Marietta Hatfield of Miami County, Ohio, to the Rotifunk mission station in Moyamba, Sierra Leone. There, Dr. Hatfield's medical work eventually led to founding a hospital. Dr. Hatfield was joined by two other medical missionaries, Dr. Mary C. Archer and Ella M. Schenck. Tragically, all three women were killed in an uprising in 1898. Yet the United Brethren in Christ were not discouraged: they sent more missionaries, rebuilt the damaged properties, and advanced the mission into more places. In 1932, Dr. Mabel Silver, from Baltimore, Maryland, was sent to Rotifunk. She described the hospital as one ward with three beds, with only herself and an interpreter as staff. They could handle twelve to fifteen mothers and babies at a time. When she retired in 1962, the maternity ward and baby clinic cared for 500-700 babies a week. In addition, 66,000 additional patients were treated annually. Unfortunately, the hospital was severely damaged in the 1992-2002 civil uprising in Sierra Leone. Recently, the government of Sierra Leone has asked United Methodists for help with Rotifunk once again. The hospital reopened with United Methodist support in 2014."

—Taken, with alterations, from Christie R. House, "House Notes: Caring for Mothers, Sierra Leone (Part 2: The Development of Rotifunk Hospital)," New World Outlook, July 2011

....

Whatever the form of mission, whoever has been engaged in it, and whatever their relationship with formal church structures, what has most characterized United Methodist mission and United Methodists in mission over the last 200 years has been a willingness to faithfully answer God's call and join in the *missio Dei*, even despite challenges, hardships, hard decisions, resistance, persecution, and other obstacles. In the Methodist understanding, mission happens when God's gracious initiative is met by a human response that says, "Here I am, send me" (Isa 6:8 NET). This willingness to answer the missionary call is shaped through and supported by prayer, Bible study, theological reading, and other spiritual practices. It is informed by the lenses of biblical, Wesleyan, and other strains of mission theology. And at its core, it reflects what is best about mission and what is best about the Wesleyan understanding of Christianity: the divine and the human, working together for the sake of the redemption of the world.

When the divine and the human are aligned in that way, amazing things can happen. Impossible hurdles can be overcome, and unbelievable good can be done. Methodist mission has endured through wars, church divisions, social upheavals, economic downturns, disease outbreaks, and its own failings because of the faithfulness of Methodist women and men from around the world who have said, "Send me," when they have heard God calling. In the process, they have preached, healed, taught, befriended, stood in solidarity with, supported, trained, empowered, advocated for, and lived among countless others, whose lives have been touched in profound ways as a result. Global Ministries prays that the stories of previous generations of faithful United Methodists will inspire future generations to say yes to God's call to mission, that God may continue to redeem the world with and through them.

44

Recommended Readings

For a good overview of mission history that both includes the broad sweep of that history and pays attention to the past two centuries of Methodist mission history, see:

- Dana L. Robert. *Joy to the World: Mission in the Age of Global Christianity.* New York: Women's Division, The General Board of Global Ministries, The United Methodist Church, 2010.

For a thorough discussion of how assumptions of racial and cultural superiority were baked into American approaches to mission starting with mission to Native Americans and running through to world mission, see:

- William R. Hutchison. *Errand to the World: American Protestant Thought and Foreign Missions.* Chicago: University of Chicago Press, 1987.

The United Methodist Church History of Mission Series edited by Charles Cole includes detailed histories of the last 200 years of mission in The United Methodist Church and its predecessors:

- Ruth A. Daugherty. *The Missionary Spirit: The History of Mission of the Methodist Protestant Church, 1830–1939.* New York: General Board of Global Ministries, The United Methodist Church, 2004.

- Linda Gesling. *Mirror and Beacon: The History of Mission of The Methodist Church, 1939–1968.* New York: General Board of Global Ministries, The United Methodist Church, 2005.

- Robert Harman. *From Missions to Mission: The History of Mission of The United Methodist Church, 1968–2000.* New York: General Board of Global Ministries, The United Methodist Church, 2005.

- J. Steven O'Malley. *"On the Journey Home": The History of Mission of the Evangelical United Brethren Church, 1946–1968.* New York: General Board of Global Ministries, The United Methodist Church, 2003.

45

- Robert W. Sledge. *"Five Dollars and Myself": The History of Mission of the Methodist Episcopal Church, South, 1845–1939*. New York: General Board of Global Ministries, The United Methodist Church, 2005.

For the history of mission of the Methodist Episcopal Church prior to 1939, the best source still remains the four-volume History of Methodist Mission series by Wade Crawford Barclay and J. Tremayne Copplestone:

- Wade Crawford Barclay. *Early American Methodism, 1769–1844*. Vol. 1, *Missionary Motivation and Expansion*. History of Methodist Mission series. New York: Board of Missions and Church Extension of the Methodist Church, 1949.

- Wade Crawford Barclay. *Early American Methodism, 1769–1844*. Vol. 2, *To Reform the Nation*. History of Methodist Mission series. New York: Board of Missions and Church Extension of the Methodist Church, 1950.

- Wade Crawford Barclay. *The Methodist Episcopal Church, 1845–1939*. Vol. 3, *Widening Horizons, 1845–1895*. History of Methodist Mission series. New York: The Board of Missions of The Methodist Church, 1957.

- J. Tremayne Copplestone. *The Methodist Episcopal Church, 1896–1939*. Vol. 4, *Twentieth-Century Perspectives*. History of Methodist Mission series. New York: Board of Global Ministries of The United Methodist Church, 1973.

CHAPTER 4

MISSION CONCEPTS AND RELATIONSHIPS, 2010-2020

Thomas Kemper

The mission bicentennial observance gives us as United Methodists both an opportunity to reflect on our past 200 years of mission and an occasion to look at what we are doing now through the General Board of Global Ministries. I have served as General Secretary of the agency for the decade leading into the bicentennial. Accordingly, what follows is an account of the agency's work over that period. This work has been informed and shaped by what we as Methodists have learned from the nearly two centuries of mission that preceded it. And I am conscious that the work we have done together over the past ten years will continue to impact United Methodist mission efforts in the years ahead. In this way, I feel strongly that it is critical to talk about mission past, present, and future together. Each informs the others.

The years 2010 to 2020 form a remarkable decade for United Methodist global ministry and mission, including the United Methodist Committee on Relief. Global Ministries has encountered and taken positive account of expected and unexpected challenges. It has made significant changes in governance, moving from a board of directors of almost one hundred members that met for a week at a time to a board of thirty-seven that can do its work in three days or by technological means. It has adopted a more regionalized operational style that includes new headquarters in Atlanta after almost 200 years in New York City. But structure and governance are not my major interests here.

My emphases here are, first, on the key mission concepts and relationships that have guided Global Ministries' work over the last decade and that now point toward the future, and, second, on specific illustrative highlights of this work for mission, which is always praxis as well as theory. I will conclude with personal impressions rooted in my experience as a missionary and agency administrator. I will use present tense verbs primarily in what follows because most of the work discussed is continuing.

Mission Concepts and Relationships

Global Ministries' work is rooted in the theological concept of the *missio Dei*—God's mission, and it is expressed through a network of collaborative relationships and an emphasis on facilitating the work of others. This pattern is evident in everything in my survey of mission highlights across the last ten years.

Global Ministries in the years in focus refined its mission theology and strengthened its practice of partnerships. The work on a theology of mission statement came at the request of directors and missionaries. In 2010, Global Ministries had two long mission theology documents from the late 1980s—one, *Grace upon Grace*, adopted by General Conference in 1988 as a denominational study paper;[1] the other, "Partnership in God's Mission," that had emerged a year or so earlier from an internal board of directors' introspection process.[2] The second was the more "practical" of the two but was overly concerned with details. Early in my time at the agency, Global Ministries moved toward a complementary new, shorter mission theology statement, attuned to the reality and vocabulary of the twenty-first century. Directors and members of the United Methodist Missionary Association were active in producing several drafts, and the final version, approved by the directors, is now widely

---

1. *Grace upon Grace: The Mission Statement of The United Methodist Church* (Nashville: Graded Press, 1990).

2. "Partnership in God's Mission: Theology of Mission Statement" (New York: General Board of Global Ministries, 1986).

used.[3] It is strong on grace, centered on the *missio Dei*, and directed toward mission in partnership.

Missio Dei

The central insight of *missio Dei* is that mission "begins with God, belongs to God, and will be fulfilled by God at the end of time."[4] God is the primary actor in mission, not an agency nor the church nor individual Christians. Global Ministries' Theology of Mission statement announces in the first paragraph, "Global Ministries is in mission to witness to what God has done and is doing, and to learn from what God is doing in every land where disciples gather in the name of Jesus Christ." The mission and the transforming power belong to God.

The statement goes on to describe God's mission from creation to completion in God's time. It affirms that the church

> lifts up the name of Jesus in thought, word, and deed, proclaiming Jesus Christ . . . through its own incarnate living. . . . By representing the revelation of God in Christ in word and deed, the Church remains faithful both to the Great Commandment that we love God with all our heart, soul, mind, and strength, and our neighbor as ourselves; and to the Great Commission that we make disciples of all nations.

The Holy Spirit, the statement reminds us, "calls the Church into being for mission"; the church "is one sign of God's presence in the world." And "the Spirit is always moving . . . the Church into a new mission age. With openness and gratitude, we await the leading of the Spirit in ways not yet seen." The phrase about the Spirit's leading is displayed prominently in the fellowship hall of Global Ministries' building in Atlanta. It is a constant reminder of the agency's engagement in God's mission. Other lines from the Mission Theology statement appear in motivational displays throughout the building.

This emphasis on God's mission appears in the literature and statements published across the last decade and is notable in the call for unity in mission ("United in God's Mission") issued in 2019 by the directors in response to

---

3. See appendix B, or "Our Theology of Mission," Global Ministries, https://umcmission.org/our-theology-of-mission/.

4. "Our Theology of Mission."

the sharp divisions in the denomination following the Special General Conference in St. Louis, an event that failed to resolve questions of inclusion of LGBTQ persons. The directors reminded United Methodists of the many ways they are in mission through missionaries, disaster response, health and education ministries, creation care and economic development. They declared, "This is God's work . . . [and] we believe that the work God has called us to do represents what is right with the global church. . . . We remain committed to the *missio Dei*."[5]

Collaboration

Significantly, in the statement "United in God's Mission," the affirmation of the *missio Dei* is immediately followed by an invitation to others "to participate in what God is already doing in saving, healing and transforming the lives of all people, everywhere in this world." This is a call to collaboration.

The concept of collaboration in mission is not new, but it has been deepened and extended in the past decade. Global Ministries' motto, "Connecting the Church in Mission," a recognition of collaboration and of the ideal of "mutuality in mission," had already come into use with the 2009–12 quadrennium and would be underscored by evolving mission mandates. The 2008 General Conference introduced the United Methodist Four Areas of Focus—leadership development, new places for new people, global health, and ministry with the poor—as denominational priorities, with general agencies given responsibility for specific areas. Global Ministries' focus was ministry with the poor. Accordingly, it provided motivational and educational resources on the topic, most notably, on the concept and praxis of ministry *with*. Ministry and mission should always be *with* others—not "to" or "for" them. "Ministry with" is now an integral part of our mission vocabulary and mindset. Global Ministries would later be assigned the focus area on global health by the Council of Bishops, and I thank God for the experience in working with the denomination to promote creative, collaborative ministry *with*—with the poor, as well as with congregations, conferences, schools, nonprofits, foundations, related Methodist denominations, and ecumenical partners—for this has informed Global Ministries' approach to the Abundant

---

5. "United in God's Mission: An Invitation from the Directors of the General Board of Global Ministries, The United Methodist Church," General Board of Global Ministries, https://www.umcmission.org/share-our-work/news-stories/2019/april/global-ministries -directors-call-for-unity-in-god-s-mission.

Health Initiative, introduced in 2016 with the goal of providing life-saving interventions for a million children.

Photo: Jennifer Silver, Global Ministries

"From the very birth of the Methodist movement, the call upon God's people has been one of mission and service. . . . Our greatest gain has been in a post-colonial awakening and greater understanding of the complexity of a diverse global faith communion. . . . We constantly engage in the shift from ministry 'to' and 'for' to ministry 'with' and 'of.' And doing ministry 'for' others is disempowering. Bringing ministry 'to' others is patronizing. But ministry 'with' opens all involved to transformative partnership. And discovering the ministry 'of' other people is empowering and life-giving. . . . The opportunities to spread the gospel have never been more abundant. . . . I hope that we can . . . all grab the Holy Spirit and say to each other, 'We are at God's moment. We are the powerful moment to transform the world.' Yes, the world is broken. Yes, this world has such a hunger for spirituality and all justice and mercy. Yet, such a potential demands much. To engage such a diverse and complex global community requires humility, grace, patience, and a gentle spirit. We go forth with a desire to offer them Christ. Not to change people or to judge people or to impose our narrative into someone else's story. We offer meaning, not a narrow and rigid truth. But what we have to offer in God's name only has value if it springs from a deep commitment to mercy and justice."

—*Bishop Hee-Soo Jung, president, Global Ministries Board of Directors, at the Methodist Mission Bicentennial Conference, Atlanta, April 2019, opening banquet*

One of Global Ministries' ecumenical partners early in the last decade contributed significantly to the agency's vocabulary and understanding of mission today. The Commission on World Mission and Evangelism of the World Council of Churches, of which The United Methodist Church is an active member, in its 2013 declaration *Together towards Life: Mission and Evangelism in Changing Landscapes*,[6] coined the phrase *mission from the margins*. The term recognizes and names a growing reality in Global Ministries' work and all mission today, disrupting long-standing assumptions. Historically, mission flowed from centers in Europe and North America to "margins," mostly in the global South. This is no longer the case. The so-called younger churches on the historical margins are now important agents of mission enthusiasm and action. Global Ministries recognizes this is essential for the future and raises serious theological and operational challenges, since the old centers still contribute and control most of the financial resources for mission. There are significant issues of parity, mutuality, and equity to work through in the years ahead. More fully reaching these goals will require considerable collaboration.

I see the productivity of collaboration in the roundtable approach to mission planning and implementation that has come to characterize Global Ministries' work in recent years. I outlined and strongly advocated for the roundtable approach in my first address to directors in 2010. It was a new idea to American ears then but not so new to people from the central conferences. I had learned about and participated in mission roundtables with colleagues in Africa when working in mission with the Germany Central Conference. I said in that address, "The model brings to the table all of those who are in partnership with a certain conference or country in order to share the work, set priorities together, and achieve as much transparency and accountability as possible."

Mission roundtables celebrate and practice the values of equality and respect and are now standard in many areas of the agency's work. Global Ministries has published guides on the organization, leadership, and even theology of roundtables[7] and held seminars for roundtable facilitators.

---

6. Jooseop Keum, ed., *Together towards Life: Mission and Evangelism in Changing Landscapes* (Geneva: World Council of Churches, 2013).

7. Amy Valdez Barker, ed., *Mission Roundtable: Trusting the Circle, Engaging with Dialogue* (Atlanta: Global Ministries, 2019), https://drive.google.com/file/d/14oByhjbAnfuBisRz9Tox cr5EwjNYkEzF/view.

• •

"A special Burundi Annual Conference session in Gitega sealed the deal on coveted and elusive unity for United Methodists in this East African nation. . . . For 12 years . . . two factions had contended for control. . . . A reconciliation team met in Harare, Zimbabwe, in August 2017. . . . The result was a memorandum of understanding signed by both parties to operate as 'one strong and vital United Methodist Church in Burundi.' 'We went to Zimbabwe with 98 percent of our issues resolved because we understood the value of unity,' . . . said Georges Nshimirimana, a lay leader. . . . 'I cannot claim that we did a great job because God was the driver of this reconciliation.' . . . [Rev. Jean Ntahoturi, the church's newly elected legal representative, added,] 'God has accomplished His mission in Burundi.'"

—*Tafadzwa Mudambanuki, "United Methodists Celebrate Unity in Burundi," United Methodist News Service, March 14, 2018*

• •

A collaborative approach to reaching decisions on mission, one that has an inclusive table of players and strives to respect all, is a blessing from God and has been proven so again and again over the last ten years of mission experience. Collaboration brought reunion to a badly divided United Methodist community in Burundi in 2018, paved the way for mission initiatives in Cameroon and Senegal to become mission districts of the Cote d'Ivoire Annual Conference, and allowed the former Alaska Missionary Conference to project itself as a mission district of the Pacific Northwest Annual Conference.

Changing Patterns of Partnership

Patterns of partnership do change over time and in response to emerging situations. Global Ministries experienced a major transition in one of its oldest and most valuable partnerships during my years here. I am referring to the administrative changes culminating in the movement of the corporate structure of United Methodist Women (UMW) from a division of the General Board of Global Ministries to that of a separate but missionally connected organization. This development, formalized in 2012, has had enormous importance for both the UMW and Global Ministries. It was also a necessary move to correct a great injustice done to women organized for mission decades ago.

Women have always been central participants in and supporters of mission in the many streams of church life that form United Methodism. While the Missionary Society of the Methodist Episcopal Church, the earliest predecessor of Global Ministries, was chartered by men, women were responsible for much of the work. Without the strong, dedicated support of the

53

New York Female Missionary Society, mission through the Missionary Society would not have grown as it did.[8]

The Woman's Foreign Missionary Society, formed in Boston in 1869, the earliest forerunner of the UMW, represented a further step forward for Methodist mission. The bold, courageous missionaries of the WFMS not only carried out invaluable work of their own; they also gave critical aid to the work of the Missionary Society around the world. Women, both those sent by women's societies and those sent by denominational societies, historically made up the majority of Methodist missionaries.

But relationship between the official denominational missionary societies and the women's mission organizations was not equal or unproblematic. Patriarchy was all too common, constraining mission of and by women, often with limits imposed by organizational structures. And so it was, in 1964, in preparation for the formation of The United Methodist Church, that the strong tradition of women's independent mission leadership established in Boston in 1869 was subordinated into a "Woman's Division" of Global Ministries. The women, in effect, lost their freedom.

....

"Global Ministries is honored to recognize our long, shared history with United Methodist Women and the long history of significant contributions by women to mission. . . . We recognize . . . that women, both those sent out by women's societies and those sent out by denominational societies, made up the majority of Methodist missionaries historically. . . . We recognize and repent of the ways in which patriarchy limited and constrained women's work and the ways in which those injustices were reflected in the formal power structures of mission organizations. . . . We reaffirm the importance of partnership in mission now and in the future, and we rejoice in the ongoing collaboration between United Methodist Women and Global Ministries. . . . We value our cooperation in missionary deployment and other collaborative programming initiatives. And as we look back on the last 150 years of shared mission history, we look forward to continuing to walk together in mission for many years to come."

—*Thomas Kemper, General Secretary, Global Ministries, at the UMW 150th Anniversary Celebration, Boston, March 23, 2019*

....

The 150th anniversary of the founding of the Woman's Foreign Missionary Society, which coincided with the Global Ministries bicentennial in 2019, provided opportunity to acknowledge and repent of the harm done to

---

8. See Susan E. Warrick, "'She Diligently Followed Every Good Work': Mary Mason and the New York Female Missionary Society," *Methodist History* 34, no. 4 (July 1996): 214–29.

women and women's work in the 1964 decision. I conveyed a message of repentance at the UMW's 150th birthday celebration in Boston and reaffirmed
the importance of partnership in mission now and in the future. I rejoice in
the ongoing collaboration between United Methodist Women and Global
Ministries and am grateful that structural separation has not meant the end
of missional cooperation.

Facilitation

Awareness of the *missio Dei* is a theological reminder that Global Ministries is a facilitator, not the owner, of mission. This truth played a role in
the agency's decision to develop a more regional operational model and to
relocate the agency headquarters from New York City to Atlanta in 2016.
Almost 200 years in a great international city, housed since the late 1950s in
a building informally called "the God box," so called because it housed offices
of many mainline Protestant denominational and ecumenical ministries, had
given Global Ministries the reputation as the possessors of United Methodist mission, distributing grants and wisdom to colonies and dependents on
behalf of Americans. That is not who or what the agency should be. Yes, it has
know-how. It has resources and connections, and the *missio Dei* bids it to use
these gifts to strengthen others. Yet, to repeat, Global Ministries is a facilitator, not the owner, of mission.

The move to Atlanta and toward regional operation—and there is still
a way to go on that—gives a new frame of reference, a new venue, to rep-
resent the agency as facilitating mission. And it facilitates better on a global
level when it works regionally. That is why Global Ministries opened an Asia-
Pacific office in Seoul, South Korea, in 2017. Global Ministries' office for
Latin America and the Caribbean, which opened in Buenos Aires in 2016,
continues through operational centers in Brazil and Honduras. An Africa regional office location awaits determination, in light of pending General Conference decisions. In Europe, Global Ministries continues to work through
the European Commission on Mission, which brings together the interests of
The United Methodist Church's central conferences and the interests of the
British, Irish, and other European Methodist churches.

Asia Methodist Mission Platform meeting, July 2019, Vietnam
Photo: Chito Mungcal, UMC Philippines

"Exciting new opportunities for Methodist church growth and service ministries in Southeast Asia [were] on the horizon through a collaborative regional approach [begun in 2018]. This was the clear message from the first meeting of the Asian Methodist Mission Platform, held . . . in Hong Kong. . . . The enthusiasm that permeated the gathering was summed up by Bishop Hwai Teik Ong of the Methodist Church of Malaysia. 'We pray that the Asian Methodist Mission Platform will become an Asian Methodist mission movement.' . . . The Rev. Sung-Che Lam, president of the Methodist Church of Hong Kong, the host for the platform meeting, was excited both by the prospects of identifying new places to start Methodist work and the possibility of building and unifying efforts around recently launched ministries. In addition to Malaysia and Hong Kong, the churches or mission groups represented include[d] the Korean Methodist Church, the Methodist Church of Singapore, United Methodist Global Ministries, The United Methodist Philippines Central Conference and the . . . World Federation of Chinese Methodist Churches."

—Thomas Kemper, "Toward a Regional Methodist Mission Approach in Southeast Asia," United Methodist Insight, *August 16, 2018*

A dramatic example of how facilitation is more effective than high-minded pronouncements comes from Asia. The Global Ministries Board of Directors went to the 2016 General Conference with a petition to set up a Provisional Central Conference in Southeast Asia and Mongolia. There was a very good, if somewhat obscure, connectional reason for the request, but we were met in Portland with a very concerned reaction from the participants attending from autonomous Methodist churches in Asia. The reaction was, in effect, "Here goes The United Methodist Church, trying to set up an American neocolonial church structure in our territory." The United Methodist Church had failed to clarify that a central conference was needed, should any of its South East Asian mission initiatives ever decide to move toward either autonomy or annual conference status. This dissatisfaction was increased by the news that Global Ministries planned to open a regional office in South Korea. Agency leadership invited the Asian Methodist leaders to Seoul for the opening of that office and to gather around a common mission table. The conversation became increasingly warmer as we heard and discussed Asian Methodist concerns. We were able to talk as partners committed to mission in Asia. From that good event came the idea, proposed by the president of the Methodist Church of Hong Kong, for an Asian Methodist Mission Platform, to explore and launch collaborative mission in Asia. Through active listening and good conversations, collaboration became possible. Global Ministries is involved, but it does not own the platform. It is one member at the table.

2018 Roundtable for Peace on the Korean Peninsula, an event hosted by the United Methodist Board of Global Ministries in Atlanta, Georgia, Nov. 9–11, 2019. From (l) to (r): James T. Laney, J. C. Park, Jimmy Carter, John Higon Eun, Hee-Soo Jung, Thomas Kemper
Photo: Hector Amador, Global Ministries

"Former U.S. President Jimmy Carter, who helped avert a crisis between North Korea and the United States in 1994, has been working for peace for the entire Korean Peninsula ever since. In his opening address at the 2018 Roundtable for Peace on the Korean Peninsula—a Nov. 9–11 event hosted by the United Methodist Board of Global Ministries—Carter commended representatives of various Methodist denominations and ecumenical organizations for their own peace efforts. 'I can't think of a more worthy comprehensive effort for the Methodist churches of the world and for the World Council of Churches together and others . . . than to work for peace in the Korean Peninsula and also particularly for peace between North Korea and the United States.'"

—*Linda Bloom and Thomas Kim, "Carter Commends Peace Efforts for Korea,"* United Methodist News Service, *November 9, 2018*

Another example of meaningful facilitation was the 2018 Roundtable for Peace on the Korean Peninsula, which Global Ministries hosted on behalf of the international Methodist family, involving the Korean Methodist Church and the World Methodist Council, as well as several United Methodist entities. A consensus statement committed participants to work collectively and in their respective churches to encourage progress toward peace. Submitted also to the US and South Korean governments, the statement encouraged an immediate and official end of the Korean War by the approval of a formal peace treaty. Grateful for this work, South Korea President Jae In Moon sent his personal greetings, and former US President Jimmy Carter brought greetings in his opening keynote remarks beginning the Roundtable proceedings. Another key speaker was James T. Laney, former US ambassador to South Korea, former Methodist missionary, and president emeritus of Emory University. For his work as a missionary, educator, and diplomat on behalf of the people of Korea, Laney received the 2019 World Methodist Peace Award from the World Methodist Council. Global Ministries hosted the event in Atlanta with the World Methodist Council in November 2019. In 2020, it took an active role in the World Council of Churches cycle of prayer and study focused on achieving a formal peace accord and reunification on the Korean Peninsula. In all these efforts, Global Ministries focused on facilitating the work already being done by others.

Concepts and Relationships in Action

Here are more examples of themes, projects, and events showing how a mission theology based on the *missio Dei*, collaboration, and facilitation have played out in action over the past decade:

Missionaries

"From Everywhere to Everywhere" describes Global Ministries' goal in the recruitment and placement of missionaries, and the agency has made great strides in that direction. Global Ministries' missionary community is thoroughly international, achieved and maintained in large measure through multiple kinds of collaboration, involving annual and central conferences, autonomous Methodist churches, ecumenical mission partners, and congregations. It is not easy to turn a slogan into an operational reality; it takes constant vigilance. The agency's "from everywhere to everywhere" policy runs headlong into national visa restrictions and travel bans, competition with other humanitarian programs, huge student debt in some countries, and changing vocational interests. Many individuals and couples called to mission today are already retired from first careers. Younger persons may be interested in time-limited careers as missionaries. This has led to very practical challenges. For instance, what is an equitable missionary pension plan for personnel retiring to India or Indiana, Liberia or Louisiana, Colombia or California? How it is possible to make active and retiree personnel policy manuals covering from everywhere to everywhere? How do missionaries even come to know one another when they are from everywhere to everywhere?

How? Through collaboration. In 2011, I believe, Global Ministries explored such practical issues and the necessary theological framework in a missionary service consultation held at Drew Theological School in New Jersey. In that meeting, participants formulated "Guiding Principles for Mission Service," which are still operative today. Many of the agency's current policies on missionary compensation and benefits were influenced by that deliberation. To build rapport among missionaries, as well as between missionaries and staff, Global Ministries implemented a proposal to hold regional missionary gatherings primarily for fellowship, renewal, and relationship building. These gatherings continue and are of great benefit to involvement in the *missio Dei*.

Collaboration can have very practical benefits. It means having friends when you need them. Global Ministries experienced this in remarkable ways in the summer of 2018, when three young missionaries were detained by government authorities in the Philippines on spurious charges of aiding subversive persons. Global Ministries organized a protest campaign of prayer and petitions—called "Tawanda Kasama No Kami!" in the Philippines and "#LetThemLeave" in other regions—that succeeded in collecting almost twenty thousand online signatures within a week on a letter urging the Philippines government to free the missionaries. And the signatures were from all continents. The central conference and the bishops in the Philippines carried much of the weight in this campaign, and the World Council of Churches and other partners provided notable assistance. This campaign would not have been so effective without this generous collaboration.

• •

"'We believe community is the way God calls us to be in mission and the way God calls the church to be in mission.' So said Kristi Painter, a Global Mission Fellow serving in mission in Philadelphia supporting medical case management for homeless men. Inspired by Acts 2:42–47, the Global Mission Fellows program is all about community and indeed collaboration. Formed in 1948, the program supports young adults, ages 20–30, who commit to work in mission for two years, either in the USA or internationally. Living in their host communities, they work collaboratively with mission partners to help create sustainable change on mission projects aimed at alleviating poverty, improving global health, increasing educational opportunity, or supporting migrants and refugees. Among recent examples, Global Mission Fellows in Zimbabwe partner with the community to coordinate, design, and monitor health programs, including maternal and child health, malaria prevention, and HIV/AIDS education. In Brazil, fellows work with partners helping children in low income communities find safe places to grow and benefit from arts, sports, computer, language skills, and dance programming. In Hong Kong, fellows provide support for research, communication, and advocacy with local organizations working with human rights for domestic workers, migration, social justice, and peace."

—*Global Mission Fellows Program Description*

• •

Collaboration plays a pivotal part in keeping the agency's young adult mission service programs vital and growing. Ten years ago, the historic US-2 and newer mission intern programs were very small. Consolidated into the Global Mission Fellows program, today there are more than one hundred young adults in two-year mission service commitments, with many participants and placements provided by partners around the world, including central conferences and mission initiatives. I had dreamed of five hundred Global Mission Fellows in the program every year, but the goal proved too complex and too costly. However, the program has greatly extended the agency's outreach, increased its cross-cultural footprint and enhanced the future leadership pool for regional and local expressions of the church.

Wisdom gained through ecumenical partnerships has strengthened the agency's theology and practice of missionary recruitment, training, and placement. I think particularly of the document "Christian Witness in a Multi-religious World: Recommendations for Conduct," issued in 2011 by the World Council of Churches, together with the Vatican and the World Evangelical Alliance.[9] The relatively short paper, developed over five years and including United Methodist participants, is a clear reminder that all Christian mission and evangelism, including the actions of missionaries, takes place in a multi-religious world and must observe certain patterns of conduct. The conduct of mission incorporates twelve principles, including acting in God's love, imitating Jesus, performing acts of service and justice, healing, rejecting violence, freedom of religion, mutual respect, renouncing false witness, ensuring personal discernment, and building interreligious relationships. I am happy to acknowledge that United Methodist mission theology, based on an understanding of the *missio Dei*, both informed and reflects these principles and, I hope, informs agency practices.

Evangelism and Church Growth

The recommendations of "Christian Witness in a Multi-religious World" have particular relevance for new and recent mission initiatives, where partners have little or no experience of Methodism. Methodists in the United States often forget that many of the central conferences and other partners in Africa, Latin America and the Caribbean, and parts of Asia have been in the Methodist family for many, many years, some for longer than a century. Still, newer mission starts are unfamiliar with Methodist ways of doing things. (I am thinking of Southeast Asia, Central Asia, Mongolia, and the Central African Republic.) This agency and its predecessors started no new overseas missions between the late 1920s and the 1980s. That is more than a half century! Yes, The Methodist Church started UMCOR, a blessing to the world, in 1940, but no new churches during this time. Because of global political and economic upheaval, a policy of mission maintenance prevailed in that era.[10]

• •

"In 2018, the Methodist Church in Cambodia celebrated its first Provisional Annual Conference. This important milestone was the culmination of an inspiring story of pan-Methodist mission collaboration, creative missionary activity, and indigenous leadership development. The United

---

9.   See http://www.worldevangelicals.org/pdf/1106Christian_Witness_in_a_Multi-Religious _World.pdf.

10.   See David W. Scott, "Commemorating Mission: History as a Means to Revival of the Missionary Spirit," Thirteenth Oxford Institute of Methodist Theological Studies, August 12–19, 2018, https://oimts.files.wordpress.com/2018/11/2018-06-scott.pdf.

Methodist mission in Cambodia began when Cambodian refugees became United Methodists in the United States. In 1998, four Cambodian-Americans were deployed as Global Ministries missionaries to Cambodia, joining other Methodist bodies such as the Korean Methodist Church, the World Federation of Chinese Methodists, United Methodists in Switzerland/France, and the Singapore Methodist Church in developing active missions. In 2004, the leadership of these Methodist bodies agreed to join to form one church and mission, working with local representatives in shaping the outreach. The Cambodia Mission Initiative focused on new church plants. Goals of church starts included the empowerment of women to engage in Christian education, ministries with street children and youth, economic development, and community health services. Additionally, the work encompassed microfinance projects. By 2020, there were 133 Methodist faith communities with 59 clergy members and 70 active lay leaders."

—*Adapted from Global Ministries Quadrennial Report, 2020*

• •

A period of "mission initiatives" began in the early 1990s with the restart of former churches in Russia and the Baltic region, areas freed by the collapse of the Soviet Union. Courage rose for new church planting in other countries formerly under totalitarian regimes, such as Central and Southeast Asia, and then spread to parts of Africa and Central America. Some of these efforts in church growth and development have flourished; others have wilted because they could not achieve the foothold required to gain self-sufficiency. Through collaboration and the building of meaningful relationships, Global Ministries has learned a lot from its mission partners about managing expectations, celebrating joys, mourning disappointments, and caring for one another. It has also learned from partners and from its past, notably from its Evangelical United Brethren ancestors, the essential importance of indigenous involvement and leadership in new mission starts. I pray that Global Ministries going forward will not undertake new mission initiatives without extensive interaction with local, regional, and international collaborators, as well as dialogue with other communions that may anticipate church starts in comparable areas.

Global Health

The story of health as a component in mission has unfolded in new ways in the past decade. Of course, health and wholeness—understood as spiritual, mental, and physical well-being—have been included in mission since the ministry of Jesus and figured prominently in the work of John Wesley. Wesley's book of home health advice, *Primitive Physick*, was an eighteenth-century bestseller (twenty-four editions in Wesley's lifetime), carried along with the Bible in the saddle bags of early English Methodist circuit riders. Accounts of missionary doctors, nurses, and technicians, as well as the hospitals and clinics they founded, fill Methodist archives.

I have welcomed in recent years two new or renewed emphases on mission and health. The first is a fresh awareness of healing as part of the theological substance of mission. By this, I mean healing in a broad Wesleyan sense, involving scientific application, humanitarian care, and spiritual exercise through prayer. Global Ministries' Theology of Mission statement recognizes this in a paragraph on "transformative witness." The text says, "The Church in Mission lifts up the name of Jesus in word and deed, proclaiming Jesus Christ as the Word become flesh through its own incarnate living; deeds of love; and service, healing, and renewal."

It is more fully developed in the ecumenical *Together towards Life*, mentioned earlier, in a section on the healing and wholeness of life, the first such highly developed treatise of this theme in any ecumenical publication on mission and evangelism. The affirmation is thrilling:

> Healing was not only a central feature of Jesus' ministry but also a feature of his call to his followers to continue his work (Matthew 10:1). Healing is also one of the gifts of the Holy Spirit (1 Corinthians 12:9; Acts 3). The Spirit empowers the church for a life-nurturing mission, which includes prayer, pastoral care, and professional health care on the one hand and prophetic denunciation of the root causes of suffering, transformation of structures that dispense injustice, and pursuit of scientific research on the other. Health is more than physical and/or mental well-being, and healing is not primarily medical. This understanding of health coheres with the biblical-theological tradition of the church, which sees a human being as a multidimensional unity and the body, soul, and mind as interrelated and interdependent. It thus affirms the social, political, and ecological dimensions of personhood and wholeness. Health, in the sense of wholeness, is a condition related to God's promise for the end of time as well as a real possibility in the present.[11]

11. *Together towards Life*, 19; quoting in part *Healing and Wholeness: The Church's Role in Health* (Geneva: WCC Publications), 1990.

The second emphasis in health and healing is Global Ministries' broad collaboration encompassing congregational, conference, ecumenical, institutional, foundation, corporate, other nonprofit, and governmental partners. This breadth is perhaps most visible in Global Ministries' work to overcome malaria and its current focus on lifesaving interventions for children. The United Methodist "Imagine No Malaria" campaign, led by United Methodist Communications and involving Global Ministries and UMCOR as critical participants, established Global Ministries and UMCOR as trusted partners with others committed to the fight against malaria. These others included the United Nations as well as philanthropies and hundreds of villages in Africa. The campaign served as one motivation for the development of conference or episcopal area health boards, predominantly in Africa, and gave a boost to the renewal of links with the United Methodist network of more than three hundred related hospitals and clinics.

"Abundant Health," the health campaign following "Imagine no Malaria," had a goal of one million lifesaving interventions for children by the end of 2020 and was also broadly collaborative, linked to local and international campaigns to address nutrition and maternal health and child concerns. Global Ministries is one of the few faith-based members of the United Nations' Every Woman, Every Child Initiative, an effort of governments, the private sector, and civil society to ensure that women, children, and adolescents are at the heart of development. It has also provided incentives for congregation-based community health programs in the United States.

Service to Those in Need

The following chapter deals with the role of diakonia (service) in God's mission, but the topic also deserves mention in this chapter's decade overview because in recent years Global Ministries has effectively interpreted and significantly tightened the relationship of mission to the work of UMCOR. This includes international and US disaster response, social and economic development, and migration, all done without regard to religion, race, nationality, gender, or sexual orientation. By greatly increasing services to migrants worldwide, the agency brought into clearer focus UMCOR's founding challenge, which was creative response to the needs of refugees and people internally displaced by conflicts in Asia and Europe during World War II. UMCOR, launched in 1940 as the Methodist Committee for Overseas Relief, was an expansion of an earlier Methodist committee organized by Bishop Herbert Welch to care for people displaced by war in China.

The number of displaced people on a global scale—including asylum seekers, refugees, and economic migrants—soared across the decade, reaching 70 million in 2020, the largest number in history.[12] Global Ministries and UMCOR in that year supported partners working in nine countries. UMCOR continues to support National Justice for Our Neighbors (NJFON), which, through affiliates in the United States, provides free or low-cost immigration legal assistance. UMCOR also assists the ecumenical Church World Service in the resettlement of refugees in the US.

UMCOR works on all continents as needed. Remarkable outreach was done in the last decade in response to major natural disasters, such as the 2010 earthquake in Haiti and the frequent storms in the Caribbean, United States, and Philippines, but also to less well-known disasters, health emergencies, and armed conflicts around the world. Partners are almost always involved for the sake of avoiding duplication and achieving maximum positive effect. The UMCOR and Global Health units collaborated with a range of regional and local partners in the Sheltering in Love response to the coronavirus pandemic that struck in 2020.

Human Rights and Religious Freedom

Global Ministries has underscored and taken in expanded directions its historic commitments to human rights and, especially, religious freedom. I acknowledge that the latter is a lifelong interest of mine. In my youth, I became aware of restrictions on the free expression of religion experienced by my Christian colleagues east of the Iron Curtain.

In the general area of human rights, I am grateful for Global Ministries' participation in the interagency Task Force on Human Rights and Investment Ethic, which it organized with the United Methodist Board of Pension and Health Benefits (now Wespath). In 2014, the task force, with members from general agencies and affiliated partners, drafted guidelines for the denomination's investments, including those of this board, so that, by policy, it would identify for its investments those "resources, principles, and procedures that express our commitment to human rights, taking into account fiduciary

---

12. "Migration," United Nations, https://www.un.org/en/sections/issues-depth/migration/index.html.

65

responsibility and ministry priorities, consistent with the global mission and ethical standards of The United Methodist Church."[13] It is no easy task to find common ground around issues involving profit, fiduciary duties, and scriptural holiness—to inject a Wesleyan theme. The task force did a commendable job. As I said at the time, "What we do as a church in mission cannot be separated from how we invest our resources. We have reached points of agreement, consensus, on how we will go about dealing with specific situations that arise in the complicated matrix of international investment and its moral implications."[14]

Religious freedom is a matter of both self-interest and an expression of love for neighbor. As Christians, we appeal to it in order to

- assert the right of Christians to share the story of Jesus, the gospel, and to form communities, that is, churches, for worship, mutual support, and acts of service to others;

- defend the rights of historic Christian groups and other faith minorities in lands where laws, politics, or culture oppress them; and,

- assure that our humanitarian services can be and are provided without regard to religious affiliation, nationality, race, ethnicity, gender, or sexual orientation.

Global Ministries has taken up the cause of persecuted and marginalized religious minorities, Christian and others, frequently during the past decade, with recurring reference to Pakistan, Nigeria, and Palestine.

Christian minorities in the majority-Muslim country of Pakistan are often targeted by extremists. And so, it happened in September 2013 that suicide bombers invaded the courtyard of All Saints Church in Peshawar right after Sunday services. The blasts killed 127 people and wounded more than 250. Among the dead were two children of Insar and Uzma Gohar and Insar's mother. Insar was the youth coordinator of the Church of Pakistan, a Global Ministries mission partner. When the Gohars spoke to the agency's direc-

13. "Draft Report," Human Rights and Investment Ethics Task Force, The United Methodist Church, 2014.

14. Quoted in Linda Bloom, "Report on Investing, Human Rights Offers Guidelines," *United Methodist News Service*, April 30, 2014.

tors while recovering in the US, their remarks were translated by a Muslim staff member originally from Pakistan. Global Ministries was able to assist in arranging to further Insar's education. After a three-year program, Insar graduated with two masters degrees from the Claremont School of Theology in California and returned to Pakistan to work in sacrificial discipleship for better interfaith relations and the welfare of his community. Global Ministries has also partnered with the Church of Pakistan to bring its schools up to required safety standards.

• •

"As Paul warned the Galatians long ago, today too many neighbors of different faiths are devouring one another rather than living together in mutual respect and love. Religious freedom seeks to restore the rule of love that binds us through our diversity, over against the ways of fear, hate, and violence that keep us divided. . . . We affirm that often we learn more about, and deepen, our own faith when we share and engage with others. . . . Our commitment to religious freedom leads us to challenge any secular or religious claim to the right to impose one religious way onto others. . . . When any religion is used to justify violence or hateful attacks on others, God mourns, and God calls us all to repent and seek an end to such violence. In humility, we affirm that God's love is too strong, too broad, and too deep for any of us to constrain or prescribe how God continues to work among us all. . . . Religious freedom, grounded in love, invites us into the hard work of dialog, listening and sharing with different faith communities, and also to acts of reconciliation across boundaries that divide."

—From "Religious Freedom: Grounded in Love," a resolution submitted to the United Methodist General Conference by Thomas Kemper for Global Ministries

• •

Along with defending religious freedom in concrete situations, Global Ministries has offered a sound theological and biblical rationale for a principle too often identified only with civil and human rights. A resolution approved by directors in 2015 and intended for consideration by the 2016 General Conference describes religious freedom as "Grounded in Love."[15] The resolution is a theology of and for religious freedom; it understands religious freedom as flowing from the grace of God. The advocacy and practice of such freedom requires attentiveness to the ebb and flow of history and to the aspirations and fears of differing communities in various cultures. It probes the admonition of Colossians 3 to "bear with one another." The resolution

---

15. The resolution is printed in full in the November/December 2016 issue of *New World Outlook*.

was resubmitted, per directors' approval, for action at the General Conference delayed from May 2020 to August 2021.

Peace and Justice in the Middle East

• •

"After a visit to the region, a delegation of Methodist representatives expressed horror at the military occupation of the Palestinian people. 'We witnessed the bitter fruits of military occupation that have fallen disproportionally upon the Palestinian people,' said a statement of the delegation, which was made up of leaders of the World Methodist Council, the British Methodist Church, and the General Board of Global Ministries of The United Methodist Church. 'We heard stories of families being separated, the denial of basic human rights, inequality of treatment, and the need for the Palestinian people to have a voice in the process of governing their own lives and future.' The group's visit marked the seventh anniversary of the opening of the Methodist Liaison Office in Jerusalem. . . . Their goal was to further the office's mission of engaging the world Methodist family in Christ's ministry of peace, truth, justice and mercy among all peoples living in the land, in partnership with the Palestinian Christian Community."

—*"Methodist Delegation Sees 'Bitter Fruits' of Palestinian Occupation," Global Ministries Communications, July 17, 2019*

• •

Global Ministries reached out in new ways to Middle East concerns, notably in Israel/Palestine. In 2012, the agency joined with the World Methodist Council and The Methodist Church in Britain in forming the Jerusalem Liaison Office for the purpose of increasing international awareness and involvement of the Methodist community in the struggle for a just peace in Israel and Palestine. The office upholds the Methodist commitment to peace and justice for both Israelis and Palestinians, including introducing Methodist pilgrims who visit the Holy Land to local Christians, indeed Palestinians, whose ancient communities are dwindling in size. This has led to renewed concern for the current and future situation of the Palestinians, including the Christian minority, and has given me personal grief, for I have come to see two valid liberation movements in deadly conflict. I say this as a German who is pro-Israel by history and upbringing but also now pro-Palestine by experience and observation. When I see what is happening to the people of Gaza and the West Bank, the people around Bethlehem, I cannot justify an uncritical pro-Israeli position. I feel the need for much more prayer and intentional international diplomacy. Interaction with the United Methodist Task Force on Israel/Palestine at Global Ministries gives me hope for the denomination's role in future conversations.

Ecumenical Mission Engagement

I want to elaborate further on ecumenical relations. Collaboration with other Christians in mission is an inherited and inherent dimension of Methodism. Global Ministries works closely on many fronts with other Methodist denominations, as well as with ecumenical organizations. Over the last two quadrennia, the agency has worked closely with the World Council of Churches and its Commission on World Mission and Evangelism, an entity originally formed as the International Missionary Council in 1921. The commission was responsible for the document *Together towards Life: Mission and Evangelism in Changing Landscapes*, formally presented to the WCC's general assembly in Busan, South Korea, in 2013. I have already shared with you the positive impact of this publication on Global Ministries' work, and since its publication, I have responded to it in several venues and journals, including giving an "ecumenical Protestant response" in a book on ecumenical missiology.[16]

Between WCC assemblies, the commission holds a major conference, most recently in 2018 in Arusha, Tanzania. Global Ministries played important roles in planning and implementing this conference on the theme "Moving in the Spirit: Called to Transforming Discipleship." The initial planning meeting was held at Global Ministries' Atlanta headquarters on my invitation as a member of the commission. The United Methodist Church had a delegation of eight at Arusha, and two Global Ministries missionaries were given organizational leadership roles as conference coordinator and as staff for the youth program.

Native American Ministries/Mission Bicentennial

The events and themes of the mission bicentennial observation are included in other chapters of this book, but I here want to underscore the im-

---

16. Thomas Kemper, "Together towards Life: An Ecumenical Protestant Assessment," in *Ecumenical Missiology: Changing Landscapes and New Conceptions of Mission*, ed. Kenneth R. Ross, Jooseop Keum, Kyriaki Avtzi, and Roderick R Hewitt (Oxford: Regnum Books, 2016), 419–28. See also Thomas Kemper, "The *Missio Dei* in Contemporary Context," *International Bulletin of Missionary Research* 38, no. 4 (October 2014): 188–90.

portant link between the anniversary and the agency's strong commitment to Native American ministries. One bicentennial moment of great significance was the return of land in Ohio held in trust for the Wyandotte people since 1843 (for more, see the chapter on "The Relationship between the Methodists and the Wyandotte"). This land comprised sacred spaces associated with the missionary John Stewart, whose ministry among the Wyandotte from 1816 to 1823 inspired the organization of the Methodist Episcopal Missionary Society in 1819.

The return of the land at Upper Sandusky, Ohio, was a glorious event of both rejoicing and repentance. It significantly reinforced Global Ministries' long-standing commitments to Native American and indigenous peoples. The agency emphasizes this as a missional priority, partly because of the guilt we as Christians and Methodists share in the horrendous sin the church has committed against Native Americans and other indigenous people over the centuries. Global Ministries vigorously supports the implementation of the United Methodist Act of Repentance with Native Peoples adopted by the 2012 General Conference. This concern figured in the move of the agency's headquarters to Georgia. Atlanta has a major league baseball club with a name and other Native American references offensive to Native Americans and opposed by The United Methodist Church. In response to this and other indigenous issues, Global Ministries developed a new working group supporting Native American sisters and brothers. The agency increased support through UMCOR for Native American communities and through such actions is building collaborative relations with Native nations in North American space.

At several points during the decade, Global Ministries made common cause with the Standing Rock Sioux and other Native Americans in opposing construction and operation of the 1,172-mile-long Dakota Access Pipeline, which threatens clean water supplies and tribal cultural sites. In 2016, Global Ministries leadership took part in protests and conducted a public awareness event at the National Center for Civil and Human Rights in Atlanta. Covered by CNN, an ABC affiliate, and NPR, the event was an important opportunity to affirm The United Methodist Church's commitment to indigenous people. Global Ministries welcomed in mid-2020 the decision of a US federal judge to shut down the pipeline pending a thorough study of its environmental impact.

Accountability and Transparency

Alertness to God's mission and effective recourse to collaboration as a means of mission participation are paralleled by an emphasis on accountability and transparency in programmatic, administrative, and financial operations. During the decade of 2010 to 2020, Global Ministries enlarged the staff of an Office of Monitoring and Evaluation, which reported to the general treasurer and chief operating officer. An independent audit committee had already been created in the previous quadrennium, and its importance in assuring transparency in all accounting matters has grown ever since.

Monitoring and evaluation is a function used in many nonprofit organizations to measure and assess performance of projects, programs, and the overall effectiveness of institutions themselves. At Global Ministries, monitoring and evaluation contributes to transparency and accountability in program and project performance and promotes data-driven decision making and effective resource allocation and reporting. It helps to keep Global Ministries, as the mission agency of The United Methodist Church, focused on goals and priorities. It holds in clear focus the agency's commitment to diversity, equity, and inclusion in employment and service provision.

The fruitfulness of monitoring and evaluation is attested not only by corporate experience but is reflective of Paul's reminder in Romans chapter 14 that all give account of themselves before God, a truth that applies to churches and their agencies as well as individuals. Monitoring, evaluating, and auditing are watchwords in the causes of integrity and obedience. These are not punitive measures when applied to persons, groups, or activities but aim to enable, equip, and sometimes, restore. Significantly, this work at Global Ministries is carried out by people of vastly different national origins and cultural backgrounds. This helps to assure that the agency and the church will not fall back into a neocolonial mentality or mode of operation. Mutuality, respect, friendship, and a sense of interdependence are required in all aspects of monitoring and evaluation and mission.

The independent audit committee provides transparency in all accounts—those within The United Methodist Church connection and those in the agency's partner Advance and ecumenical networks. It guarantees that funds are expended as authorized and reports are received in a timely fashion. In a significant development, it was this independent committee that alerted the church to serious irregularities in financial reports from an episcopal area

71

in Africa. These systemic and regional problems continue to be pursued in conjunction with other general agencies.

Personal Impressions

Thomas Kemper
Photo: Anthony Trueheart, Global Ministries

Finally, I want to offer a few personal reflections on the questions of how ten years at Global Ministries has affected me and how the job has changed me. Those are not easy questions to answer, but I have reflected on them and want to record a few remarks in reply. My work here has made the world larger for me. I already knew the earth and its people comprise a vast world of diversity—diverse cultures, languages, ethnicities, nationalities, and religions, not to mention the diversity of hopes, dreams, likes, and dislikes. I just did not know how big it is. Such a wonderful experience it is to encounter God's vast creation and the wideness of the human family. Most of my new learning about the world and its people has been pleasant and joyful. A few incidents in my travels have been scary, such as being in the Istanbul airport when it was bombed by terrorists, but even that horror put me in touch with wonderful people, such as the Muslim family trying to get home to Somalia, part of a group with whom I was evacuated from the damaged airport.

72

That experience and many others lead me to my second point. My work here has made the world smaller for me. There is such commonality among God's diverse people. The Somalian refugee family at the Turkish airport just wanted to be home with loved ones. I, a German United Methodist living in Georgia, just wanted to be home with loved ones. My experience in the Istanbul airport attack provided opportunity to experience our shared humanity.

The commonalities of our species, I think, outweigh the dissimilarities we may have. Perhaps the great lesson of the coronavirus pandemic of 2020 is that of shared humanity. COVID-19 strikes celebrities as well as ordinary people. Yes, in the United States, it hit African American and Latino communities harder than Caucasians, and hit older people hardest, but the virus has left no group unaffected. It frightens the poor and the rich. It exempts no national or ethnic distinctions and is not "the China virus." The threat is shared by all humanity; when a vaccine or cure comes, beyond the horizon at the time of this writing, it must be made available to the entire human family. A part of our responsibility as Christians, as United Methodists, is to work for equity and justice in the care of all who suffer.

The coronavirus epidemic and panic has called United Methodists to question our immediate denominational priorities and plans. Given the enormity of the global health crisis, including enormous fear among millions, a question arises: Is our best path to holiness by way of decisions that would divide the denomination and threaten our work as United Methodists? Is that the road God is calling us to walk? I leave it as an open question, while I am very convinced that Global Ministries is prepared for whatever structural future The United Methodist Church might choose.

I have been strengthened and reassured across my decade at Global Ministries by the words to a German song, "Vertraut den neuen Wegen" ("Trust the New Ways"), written by a theology professor for a wedding, but closely associated with the breaching of the Berlin Wall on November 9, 1989, an event of pivotal importance in my faith journey.

Let me provide a context for the song. I had close ties with Christians, especially Methodists, in East Germany starting in 1975. I visited there at least twice a year to speak in churches and meet friends. I learned that the churches were the only independent organizations in the country and had a social relevance far beyond liturgies in sanctuaries. It is no surprise that East German Christians were essential to the movement that brought down the wall. We would sing the hymn projecting new ways. One communist figure said with great insight, "We had planned for everything . . . but not for candles and prayers."[17]

I came to Global Ministries as a missionary believing in the power of candles and prayers and hymns. I am still a missionary; I still believe in the power of candles and prayers and hymns. I have learned to put full trust in God's grace. I believe that Christians can change the world and that United Methodists can be transformed by the love of God. I cling to the power of the hymn's words of faith and hope, of trust and confidence:

> Have faith in God who leads you on pathways you do not know.
> To live is to set forth on new ways you dare to go.
> Whene'er God's rainbow radiant doth high in heaven stand:
> It beckons men and women: Come to the Promised Land.[18]

Are we as United Methodists prepared for the Holy Spirit to move us into a new day of mission?

Recommended Readings

Theological resources on important contemporary mission theology concepts such as *missio Dei*, collaboration, and facilitation include the following:

- *Grace upon Grace: The Mission Statement of The United Methodist Church.* Nashville: Graded Press, 1990.

- Various authors have contributed to a reevaluation of *Grace upon Grace* on the blog *UM & Global.* See http://www.umglobal.org/2020/09/um-global-collection-grace-upon-grace.html.

- Jooseop Keum, ed. *Together towards Life: Mission and Evangelism in Changing Landscapes.* Geneva: World Council of Churches, 2013.

---

17. Horst Sindermann, former GDR official. See Alexander Faludy, "We Had Planned for Everything . . . but Not for Candles and Prayers," *Church Times*, Nov. 8, 2019, https://www.churchtimes.co.uk/articles/2019/8-november/features/features/we-had-planned-for-everything-but-not-for-candles-and-prayers.

18. Klaus Peter Hertzsch, "Vertraut den neuen Wegen." Translation by Jorge Lockward.

- David W. Scott. *Crossing Boundaries: Sharing God's Good News through Mission.* Nashville: Wesley's Foundery Books, 2019.

- "Our Theology of Mission." Global Ministries. https://umc mission.org/our-theology-of-mission/. See also appendix B in this volume.

For more on how these principles play out in the work and ministry of Global Ministries, see:

- "News & Stories." Global Ministries. https://umcmission.org /news-and-statements/.

- "Our Work." Global Ministries. https://umcmission.org/our -work/.

- "Learn about Global Ministries." Global Ministries. https:// www.umcmission.org/learn-about-us.

- "Remembering, Serving, Preparing: A Mission Anniversary Quadrennium: Report of the General Board of Global Ministries to the 2020 General Conference." Global Ministries. https://umcmission.org/general-conference-2021/.

MISSION AND DIAKONIA

Thomas Kemper

S ome aspects of mission have been part of Global Ministries' work since early days, but the agency's understanding of them has unfolded slowly over time. Diakonia—service—is one of these aspects. It is an essential dimension of God's mission, although it does not receive as much popular missiological or theological interpretation as areas such as evangelism, spiritual formation, and church growth. Originally a Greek term, diakonia is typically defined as acts of goodwill and charity, as humanitarian response to need, and as duty to the downtrodden, perhaps offered in part out of a sense of guilt. The word is used throughout the New Testament, and, while it is not as familiar as terms such as *missio Dei*, it is an important term in contemporary theological reflection about service, and is the root of terms such as *deacon* and *deaconess*.

Our storytelling about diakonia is often partial. Take the account of the steps taken at the 1940 Methodist General Conference toward setting up what is today the United Methodist Committee on Relief (UMCOR), a major collective expression of Christian service. United Methodists love the familiar story: spurred on by heroic leaders, the church pragmatically acted "for the relief of human suffering," namely, the care of persons made homeless by wars in Asia and Europe, stipulating that funds raised would be used without regard to religion, race, or national origin. It is stirring but not the whole story.

". . . hungry, and ye fed me"

MCOR Feeding Chinese War Refugees, 1945
The Methodist Committee for Overseas Relief channeled much of its funding to China in its first five years. A strong Methodist Church in China at the time still hosted significant numbers of US missionaries. Drought, famine, and the invasion of Japanese troops created multiple hardships. MCOR worked with other Protestant relief agencies to provide basic necessities.
Photo: 1945 MCOR collection, General Commission on Archives and History

"Herbert Welch originated, and from 1940 to 1948, led the United Methodist Committee on Relief, or UMCOR. In the manner of Christ, he established UMCOR's work 'without distinction for race, creed, or color.' He proposed forming the agency, first called the Methodist Committee for Overseas Relief, to the 1940 General Conference to help provide immediate relief to war refugees in the Asia region. By 1942, in addition to refugee relief, the agency embraced reconstruction, rehabilitation, repatriation of refugees and prisoners of war, restoration of churches and civil operations, and reconciliation. Originally from New York, Welch played other roles significant in the church's missional, social, and institutional history. In 1905, he became president of Ohio Wesleyan University, and while there, to oppose child

Photo: General Commission on Archives and History

78

labor, he helped launch what is today the United Methodist Federation for Social Action. He was author of the first Methodist Social Creed. As mission bishop of the Methodist Episcopal Church in Japan and Korea, 1916–1928, he helped shape the affirmation of faith known as 'The Korean Creed.' Later, he served the Shanghai Area in China."

—Adapted from Elliott Wright, "Welch, Herbert (1862–1969)," Methodist Mission Bicentennial Website, https://methodistmission200.org /welch-herbert-1862-1969/

••

Setting up the Methodist Committee for Overseas Relief (MCOR, the original name) was an act of mission, a projection of the church. While there was no study commission report on the biblical roots of compassion, there was an assumption, as historian Benjamin L. Hartley has put it, that "relief related to mission—somehow."[1] This chapter is about that "somehow"—about the theology of diakonia.

It would take time to clarify the rationale for "relief" as "mission," and in a fine paper on the history of MCOR from 1940 to 1968, Hartley explores the tension as it existed. Into the 1950s, he notes, internal educational material would explain the differences between relief and missions, the latter being about gospel proclamation and "relief" as a kind of supplement.[2] Time and experience would bring the two into creative interaction.

Service Incarnates Grace

Even in 1940, it was predictable that MCOR would become linked to the then Board of Missions and Church Extension, and that the relief agency would influence mission concepts and praxis. "The alleviation of human suffering" would emerge as a formal United Methodist mission goal. Service would become recognized as a mark of mission. The Global Ministries' Mission Theology statement, adopted in 2011, stipulates that "deeds of love; and service, healing, and renewal"[3] are signs of Christ incarnate in the church and are closely aligned with proclamation and teaching as bearers of God's grace.

---

1. Benjamin L. Hartley, "'For the Relief of Suffering': The Methodist Committee for Overseas Relief in the Context of Cold War Initiatives in Development, 1940–1968," *The Methodist Review* 6 (2014): 38, https://www.methodistreview.org/index.php/mr/article /view/100aHrHaHartH.

2. Hartley, "For the Relief of Suffering," 39ff.

3. See appendix B, or "Our Theology of Mission," Global Ministries, https://umcmission .org/our-theology-of-mission/.

This line of thought begins in the scriptures, but too often, like the traveler in the parable of Luke 10, has been left lying by the side of the road.

That concern for those in distress is more than kindness and is rooted in both the Old and New Testaments. It has its roots in holiness—a concept that is both thoroughly biblical and distinctively Methodist. As Rabbi Myrna Matsa observes, the people of God "accept in perpetuity the rule of law established by the Divine. Leviticus 19:2, 'You shall be holy because I the Lord your God am holy,' is followed by 36 verses that explain in concrete terms what it means to be holy. . . . We serve God by nurturing the earth, caring for humanity, and leaving the world in a better condition than the way we found it."[4]

Jesus was steeped in the Jewish tradition of holiness and acknowledged the care and nurture of humanity as the outpouring of divine grace. Matthew 25 spells out the ethics of diakonia—to the hungry, thirsty, sick, unclothed, or in prison. In the Great Commandment, Jesus tells us to love and care for our neighbors as we care for ourselves—an admonition also from the Old Testament—and in Galatians 5:14 (NRSV), the Apostle Paul cites, "You shall love your neighbor as yourself," as the summary of the whole of religious law.

· ·

"Christ's love may come in the form of one, who helps turn our lives from self-serving and self-seeking to ones that reach out to others. Love may come in the form of a tent, a blanket, a new house, a job, a new community, and a new life for those who have been uprooted or displaced. This love may come in the form of bread, wheat, rice, legumes, green leafy vegetables for physical bodies. . . . It may come in the form of water—a well, a pipe, a dam that sustains life. . . . This love may come in the form of someone who hears our story, shares our pain, our poverty, works to make changes in systems that enslave; it never abandons us. When we are touched by God's love, we are changed forever.

"For fifty years, UMCOR has been an important link in many lives touched by God's love through Christ. Once touched by God's love, our lives, our community, and our church are never the same."

—*Norma Kehrberg, former Deputy General Secretary of UMCOR (1984-1991),* Love in Action: UMCOR; 50 Years of Service *(Nashville: Abingdon, 1989), 31-32.*

· ·

Acts 11 tells the story of what may have been the first Christian collection for disaster survivors. When the church in Antioch learned that fellow believers in Judea faced famine, "the disciples determined that according to their

---

4. Myrna Matsa, "Jewish Theology of Disaster and Recovery," *Neshama*: Association of Jewish Chaplains (NAJC), http://jewishchaplain.net/wp-content/uploads/2018/09/h_Theology_of_Disaster_Response_and_Recovery.pdf.

ability, each would send relief to the believers living in Judea" (Acts 11:29, NRSV). Yet for Jesus, the realm of neighborliness went beyond familiarity. In the story of the Good Samaritan in Luke 10, Jesus broadens the definition of a "neighbor," cutting across ethnic and religious boundaries for the sake of human service and dignity.[5]

Wesleyan Heritage

John Wesley, the eighteenth-century English founder of Methodism, had high theological and practical regard for diakonia. He advocated acts of mercy for people in jeopardy because of natural or human-caused calamities. Service for Wesley also embraced advocacy. He deplored and sought to counteract some of the unhealthy and unsafe results of rapid industrialization such as child labor. He strongly opposed slavery and the slave trade. Wesley was also an early ecologist. He warned against pollution of the air, water, and soil and innovated with small enterprise programs to rescue at least some women and children from the mills. Wesley's ministry extended to those sick from all causes, including industrial contamination. Medicine was not highly developed in his time. Germs and microbes had not been identified, and existing health services were largely limited to the wealthy. Despite the many demands on his time, Wesley compiled the best available medical information, including home remedies, in a book entitled *Primitive Physick*.

Wesley held deep concern for the poor and sought to identify the causes and possible correctives for poverty. His 1772 publication "Thoughts on the Present Scarcity of Provisions"[6] condemned those who profited off the efforts of others. Many were hungry, he said, because there was no meat, and there was no meat because there was no work; no work because of inflation and bad economic conditions, which he attributed to high taxes, war, a high national debt, and luxurious living. He also had harsh words for those who syphoned off grain for the distilling of strong drink. "Many thousands poor people [*sic*] are starving," Wesley wrote. What to do about it? He advised, "Find them work, and you will find them meat. They will then earn and eat their own

---

5. For the missional significance of the boundary-crossing story of Luke 10, see chapter 2 of David W. Scott, *Crossing Boundaries: Sharing God's Good News in Mission* (Nashville: Wesley's Foundery Books, 2019).

6. John Wesley, *The Works of John Wesley*, vol. 11, *The Appeals to Men of Reason and Religion and Certain Related Open Letters*, ed. Gerald R. Cragg (Nashville: Abingdon Press, 1989).

bread."[7] But how were employers to create jobs "without ruining themselves?" Wesley's solution was as follows: by providing as much work as can be done, laborers will not only be able to buy meat but will earn and thus spend money for other things that profit the "masters." Whether Wesley was a good economist is not relevant. What matters is his understanding that Christian service includes evaluation of social and economic conditions and efforts to shape just policies and practices of benefit to the general population. This includes distribution of resources.

• •

"We commonly mean by that expression [means of grace], those that are usually termed, works of piety; viz., hearing and reading the Scripture, receiving the Lord's Supper, public and private prayer, and fasting. . . . But are they the only means of grace? . . . Surely there are works of mercy, as well as works of piety, which are real means of grace. . . . And those that neglect them, do not receive the grace which otherwise they might. . . . The walking herein is essentially necessary, as to the continuance of that faith whereby we are already saved [by] grace, so to the attainment of everlasting salvation. Of this [we] cannot doubt, if we seriously consider that these are the very words of the great Judge himself: 'Come, ye blessed children of my Father, inherit the kingdom prepared for you from the foundation of the world. For I was hungry, and ye gave me meat: Thirsty, and ye gave me drink: I was a stranger, and ye took me in: Naked, and ye clothed me: I was sick, and ye visited me: I was in prison, and ye came unto me.' (Matt. 25:34, &c.) 'Verily, I say unto you, Inasmuch as ye have done it to the least of these my brethren, ye have done it unto me.'"

—*John Wesley, "On Visiting the Sick," 1786. Available from the Wesley Center Online at http://wesley.nnu.edu/john-wesley/the-sermons-of-john-wesley-1872-edition/sermon-98-on-visiting-the-sick/*

• •

But diakonia for Wesley was more than mercy and compassionate intentions. Service was a "means of grace," that is, a means of God at work through the church and believers in the world. As means of grace, acts of mercy—individual and communal—are sacramental in Wesleyan thought. Wesley saw practicing acts of mercy as an important way by which Christians could grow in love for others. Wesley termed this growth in love "holiness." Wesley believed that growth in holiness should be the focus of the Christian life.

---

7. John Wesley, "Thoughts on the Present Scarcity of Provisions," *The Works of John Wesley* (Grand Rapids: Zondervan Publishing House, n.d.), 11:353–54, quoted in Thomas William Madron, "Some Economic Aspects of John Wesley's Thought Revisited," *Methodist History* 4, no. 1 (October 1965): 40.

Wesley's regard for service as the word of God at work in the world pre-figures the more contemporary thought of the late Nikois Nissiotis, one of few modern-day theologians to address the role of service in mission. Nis-siotis, a Greek professor and basketball coach, was particularly interested in the ecumenical implications of diakonia. In a 1961 article in *The Ecumenical Review*, he rightly insists that diakonia "is neither a good moral act springing from the goodwill of a regenerated Christian nor an expression of compassion for the misery of man outside the Church." He continues,

> The care of the Churches for the world is not a vehicle for showing compas-sion for the suffering or the weak or the uneducated man. The help of the Churches offered to the world is not of a humanistic nature. The Churches are not primarily philanthropic institutions. The act of the diakonia of the Churches is ecclesial, namely it is the overflowing of the grace which binds and moves their inner life as a total fellowship. In other words, diakonia to the world is the echo in the world of the Word of God already accomplished in the charismatic Church.[8]

Diakonia on the part of the church bears grace for the whole world. This is a theology, a missiology, in harmony with Wesleyan vision.

In Wesleyan terms, all people need the grace of God to be redeemed, and grace is available to all, whether they become Christian or not. The mission of offering grace understands that witness and service (*Zeugnis und Dienst* in my na-tive German) are inseparable. The two are bound together as, likewise, are word and deed, evangelism and social action, confession and dialogue. The unity of witness and service has special application for missionaries or mission teams who set out to do "good works." It is a reminder that the helpers—be they cleanup crews or funders—are not superior in divine favor to those being assisted. To fol-low Jesus in servanthood to others is to be baptized in humility, seeking in con-fident modesty not to feel or look good, but to put faith into action in ways that contribute to human welfare, peace, justice, and reconciliation—for all. Indeed, Nissiotis referred to "Diakonia as a church event as the Eucharist incognito."[9]

---

8. N. A. Nissiotis, "The Ecclesiological Significance of Inter-church Diakonia," *The Ecu-menical Review* 13, no. 2 (1961): 191.

9. Nissiotis, "The Ecclesiological Significance of Inter-church Diakonia," 192.

Theological Guidelines for Sharing

Nissiotis wrote in the context of ecumenical, or what he called "inter-church," diakonia, and it has been within the ecumenical movement that Christian service to the world has been most creatively explored as a matter of discipleship and mission. Diakonia is a notable theme in the work of the World Council of Churches (WCC) and represents practical opportunities for churches of different histories, polities, and theologies to find common ground in action—in service for the whole people of God.

A large ecumenical literature on diakonia exists. My introduction to it came with the WCC-related World Consultation on Ecumenical Sharing of Resources in El Escorial, Spain in 1987. This event produced "Guidelines for Sharing"[10] that both reflect and have influenced ways in which UMCOR and Global Ministries approach disaster relief, health ministries, agricultural and livelihood programs, social and economic development, and ecology. Naturally, collaboration—partnership—is a pivotal principle.

The guidelines from El Escorial reflect "a value system based on justice, peace and the integrity of creation." They recognize as partners in the use and sharing of resources "those who have been marginalized by reason of sex, age, economic and political condition, ethnic origin and disability, and those who are homeless, refugees, asylum-seekers and migrants." Emphases fall on fairness for the poor, women, and youth and equity between North and South.

Significantly, direct service ministries and the understanding of the need for justice in resource sharing at Global Ministries and UMCOR were already turned in the direction of the ecumenical guidelines set forth in 1987. From its outset in 1940, UMCOR offered assistance without regard to religion, race, nationality, politics, or gender. As an expression of diakonia, the work began with a focus on refugees and migrants—prominent in the El Escorial guidelines—caused by warfare, but the scope of work would expand to include all those made homeless through armed conflicts, as well as natural disasters and medical crisis, such as the Ebola epidemic in West Africa in

---

10.   World Council of Churches, "Guidelines for Sharing," World Consultation on Ecumenical Sharing of Resources, El Escorial, Spain, 1987. https://www.oikoumene.org/en /resources/documents/wcc-programmes/justice-diakonia-and-responsibility-for-creation /ecumenical-solidarity/guidelines-for-sharing.

2014 and the coronavirus pandemic of 2020. Natural disaster response in the United States would be added in the 1970s, expanded from the original "overseas" focus.

Now eighty years old, UMCOR is an expression of faith, a confirmation of Methodists' Christian discipleship, and a witness to our love for our neighbors. It does not distribute food, water, blankets, flood buckets, and health kits, or rebuild shelters and schools with the objective of converting others either to Christianity or to Methodism. Such a goal would miss the point of God's grace, which is offered without any strings attached. Disasters are opportunities for service—diakonia—inviting Methodists to our highest levels of compassion and concern.

Especially in the last thirty years, UMCOR's work has increasingly reflected the ecumenical goals and resource sharing principles of El Escorial. In almost every instance of natural disaster—large or small—it works with partners, some religious, others secular. Collaboration multiplies effort and avoids duplication, but it also serves a theological objective; it is not solely, perhaps not primarily, humanitarian. It is an expression of United Methodist presence—and of God's presence—in whatever is taking place in the world; it recognizes the fullness, the wholeness, of God's created order and the importance of working with others in the restoration and preservation of all creation, including human families and communities. As the Global Ministries' Theology of Mission statement says, "The church experiences and engages in God's mission as it pours itself out for others, ready to cross every boundary to call for true human dignity."

There is a clear theological and missional reason why UMCOR is part of Global Ministries. It has sometimes been suggested that UMCOR could be spun off from the mission agency. Were that to be done, Global Ministries would, out of theological necessity, have to form a new direct service and relief unit. Methodist mission requires witness and service. To repeat an affirmation from Bishop Hector F. Ortiz-Vidal of the Methodist Church of Puerto Rico, "Global Ministries and UMCOR are the two wings of the same bird."

Roland Fernandes—UMCOR Executive Committee
Photo: Jennifer Silver, Global Ministries

"I have been involved with UMCOR and Global Ministries for over twenty five years and have been so used to the uniquely crafted fabric that Global Ministries and UMCOR together create that the thought of separation of the two is not easy for me to comprehend. In my view, there needs to be a close relationship between the mission and relief and development arms of the church, and this is best exemplified in how Global Ministries and UMCOR work together. The reciprocity of the relationship—Global Ministries providing a missional and relational context to enable UMCOR's work in various areas around the world, and UMCOR being there to help a humanitarian crisis in a mission field—is unique. Development work helps sustain and enable mission, and the reverse is also true. In addition, the shared services between Global Ministries and UMCOR, ranging from finance to communications to fundraising, among others, benefit both organizations financially and in terms of effectiveness. I am grateful to be part of this unique relationship that for decades has been a huge benefit to the church."

—Roland Fernandes, General Secretary, Global Ministries and UMCOR

Diakonia Is Open-Ended Commitment

Service as an expression of mission is not a project, program, or series of such. Diakonia is open-ended commitment to life sustaining and healing purposes. When UMCOR responds to civilian casualties in a war or to survivors of a tsunami, no time frame is set for the assistance. The agency's work in response to the prolonged war in Bosnia in the late twentieth century lasted for years after hostilities ceased, covering a full decade and involving the restoration of farms and other means of livelihood and the reconstruction of the social fabric. More than a decade went into post–civil war efforts in Sudan and South Sudan and twice that in the Democratic Republic of the Congo. Service for refugee communities, such as in the Middle East, notably with Palestinians, can continue for decades. Follow-up to the 2005 Hurricane Katrina in Louisiana and the Gulf Coast in the US went on for years, including housing rehabilitation by volunteers, job training, and relocation of persons or families to start over in new places.

Photo: UMCOR photos, General Commission on Archives and History

"J. Harry Haines, a native of New Zealand, was a missionary in China and Malaysia for 21 years, an ecumenical relief executive, and for years the director and major promoter of the United Methodist Committee on Relief. He advocated for those in need and for education about the impact of poverty and political oppression affecting millions of people. Haines strongly supported economic self-development of people in poor countries and among the marginalized in more affluent regions. In 1984, after his retirement, Haines appealed to the church to 'realize that we're living in a bitterly divided world [and] we have limited resources; therefore, we have to be specialists in designated areas in the least developed countries.' Overcoming that divide was for Haines a part of mission. 'He . . . loved nothing more than to visit congregations to tell them the story of how the church responds to disasters and humanitarian needs,' said Randy Day, Global Ministries' General Secretary, 2002–2007."

—Adapted from Elliott Wright, "Haines, J. Harry (1917–2007)," Methodist Mission Bicentennial Website, https://methodistmission200.org /haines-j-harry-1917-2007/

The commitment incorporates two interrelated approaches, one aimed at care for basic human needs such as food, water, clothing, shelter, and sanitation, and the other responsive to social rights, including education, jobs/work, and political and cultural participation, which encompasses religious expression. The needs approach and the rights approach to development must travel the same course, as do justice and mercy in Jewish and Christian theology.

Achievement of the goals in response to both types of needs requires more than money and access. It also requires the skills of economic and community development. Not surprisingly, more and more emphasis in UMCOR responses goes to development, which until recently was called "rehabilitation," a term that carries with it the connotation of restoration. Development may restore—buildings, stores, shrines, and so forth—but is broader and often points toward new possibilities. Maybe what is needed after a tsunami is not the old town by the sea but a new town on the hill. True development in the spirit of diakonia requires social justice, empowerment, and healing of communities and persons. The objective is just, participatory, and sustainable, as expressed in the ecumenical call for justice, peace, and the integrity of creation.

The church promotes and contributes to such a society by keeping a clear focus on its calling to bring healing, liberation, and reconciliation to the whole world, that is, to be the channel for the message of God's salvation. In Matthew 28, Jesus, in what is called the Great Commission, charges the disciples to take the good news to the "whole"—all of the—world. This is where John Wesley found his world parish. And it is the entire world God loves in John 3:16. The ecumenical guidelines for resources sharing from El Escorial summarize a biblical truth:

> Out of abundant and outgoing love, God has created the world, and has given it to all humanity for faithful use and sharing. As recipients of God's gift of life, we are called to see the world through God's eyes, offering it in blessing through our own acts of love, sharing and appropriate use.[11]

God's grace and love is poured out for the whole world and all its people, not just for the church. The church is a means of announcing and sharing God's love in the mission of witness and service. When the church shares

---

11. World Council of Churches, "Guidelines for Sharing."

these two—witness and service—together with the world, then we are a means of grace to the world and are ourselves blessed by God's grace.

Recommended Readings

For a more extensive history of UMCOR, see:

- Benjamin L. Hartley. "'For the Relief of Suffering': The Methodist Committee for Overseas Relief in the Context of Cold War Initiatives in Development, 1940–1968." *The Methodist Review* 6 (2014): 38. https://www.methodistreview.org/index.php/mr/article/view/100.

- Norma Kehrberg. *Love in Action: UMCOR; 50 Years of Service.* Nashville: Abingdon, 1989.

The deaconess movement has a long history of combining mission and service. The theology supporting that movement is one of diakonia. For more on the deaconess movement, see:

- Mary A. Dougherty. *My Calling to Fulfill: Deaconesses in the United Methodist Tradition.* New York: Women's Division, General Board of Global Ministries, The United Methodist Church, 1997.

For more on John Wesley, his theology, and diakonia as a means of grace, see:

- Henry H. Knight. *John Wesley: Optimist of Grace.* Eugene, OR: Cascade Books, 2018.

- Paul Wesley Chilcote. *Recapturing the Wesleys' Vision: An Introduction to the Faith of John and Charles Wesley.* Downers Grove, IL: InterVarsity Press, 2009.

- David Martin Whitworth. *Missio Dei and the Means of Grace: A Theology of Participation.* Eugene, OR: Pickwick Publications, 2019.

For ecumenical perspectives on diakonia, see:

- Stephanie Dietrich, Knud Jorgensen, Kari Karsrud Korslien, and Kjell Nordstokke. *Diakonia as Christian Social Practice: An Introduction.* Eugene, OR: Wipf & Stock Publishers, 2015.

- Isabel Apawo Phiri. "An Overview on the Imperative of Diakonia for the Church." World Council of Churches, 2018. https://www.oikoumene.org/en/resources/documents/wcc -programmes/diakonia/an-overview-on-the-imperative-of -diakonia-for-the-church.

- World Council of Churches. "Theological Perspectives on Diakonia in 21st Century." World Council of Churches, 2012. https://www.oikoumene.org/en/resources/documents/wcc -programmes/unity-mission-evangelism-and-spirituality/just -and-inclusive-communities/theological-perspectives-on -diakonia-in-21st-century.

CHAPTER 6
THE RELATIONSHIP BETWEEN THE METHODISTS AND THE WYANDOTTE

David W. Scott

The power of narrative stands at the heart of this volume, and the story of John Stewart and the Wyandot[1] and other partners with whom he worked—William Walker Sr., Catherine Walker, Jonathan Pointer, Mononcue, Between-the-Logs, and others—is a central one for Global Ministries as it celebrated its bicentennial. But this story is a beginning, not an end. As other chapters in this book have shown, the story of Methodist mission, which John Stewart's story inspired, has continued for 200 years. The story of the Wyandotte, too, which long predates John Stewart's arrival, has also continued long after his coming among them. And the relationship between the two—between Methodists and Wyandotte—has also continued. New chapters continue to be written in each of these stories, and old chapters are retold and heard anew.

This chapter will share some threads of these stories—the story of the Wyandotte (including those who became Methodist), the story of Methodists

---

1. Spellings of the tribe's name vary. Most historical sources use *Wyandot* or *Wyandott*. The present-day federally recognized tribe, as well as many other contemporary sources, use *Wyandotte*. In this chapter, I will use *Wyandot* for the tribe until the twentieth century and *Wyandotte* (or the official name of the group) to refer to the tribe in recent decades.

in Upper Sandusky, Ohio, and the story of Methodists throughout the United States—as they have unfolded in past years and continue to intersect. These stories developed in the context of white American appropriation of native land and violence against Native Americans, African Americans, and others, and this oppression must be named. But these stories are also stories of agency and resilience by the oppressed and stories of Christian love and friendship among Native Americans, African Americans, and white Americans.

The Wyandot and the Methodists in Ohio

Chief Mononcue, Wyandot leader and licensed preacher of the Methodist Episcopal Church. *Etching: Paradise Del., T. D. Booth, Eng. Printer E. C. Middleton. From James B. Finley, Pioneer Life in the West. 1854. Scanned from book. Public Domain.*

John Stewart came at a time when affairs were somewhat unsettled for the Wyandot. Their foremost chief, Chief Tarhe, had recently died, and the Northwest Territory was changing—politically, economically, and demographically—in the wake of the War of 1812. While Stewart was with the Wyandot, they were negotiating the Treaty at the Foot of the Rapids (1817) and the Treaty of St. Mary's (1818), which would set the boundaries of the "Grand Reserve"—the main parcel of land on which the United States recognized Wyandot ownership.

Stewart's new religious message further unsettled matters. But his message found an audience, perhaps because of how unsettled things were. Starting in February 1817, several prominent Wyandot converted to Methodism. Their names are still recorded on the outer wall of the Wyandot Mission Church in Upper Sandusky—Matthew Peacock, Between-the-Logs, John Hicks, Mononcue, Bigtree, Squire Grey Eyes, Summundewat, Harrahoot, John Barnett, Adam Lumpy, John Solomon, Jacquis, and Little Chief. Others followed.

Chief Between-the-Logs
Etching: Paradise Del., T. D. Booth, Eng. Printer E. C. Middleton. From James B. Finley, Pioneer Life in the West. 1854. Scanned from book. Public Domain.

To secure their religious care, the Wyandot sought closer relationships with the Methodists. John Stewart obtained official recognition for his work among them, becoming licensed as a local preacher by a quarterly conference of the Ohio Annual Conference. And Between-the-Logs took the initiative to ask the Ohio Annual Conference to help the Wyandot establish a school and a church. The Ohio Annual Conference responded by sending ordained white ministers, starting with Rev. James Montgomery in 1819. Rev. James B. Finley was the most significant early Methodist minister among the Wyandot. He arrived in 1821 and continued to visit and stay until 1827. It was under his leadership that the school opened in the summer of 1823, just months before John Stewart died in December of that year. A stone church, the Wyandot Mission Church, was completed the following year.

The stone church saw a generation of Wyandot worshipping as Methodists in what is now Upper Sandusky, Ohio. Three Methodist bishops and a couple dozen Methodist ministers preached at the church between 1824 and 1843, along with numerous Wyandot preachers. A generation of Wyandot children were educated in the Methodist school, learning a curriculum taken from white sources but under Wyandot control. This was part of a larger attempt by the Wyandot to craft a new way of life for themselves that incorporated elements of white culture—such as agricultural practices—but on Wyandot terms. The Wyandot hoped, with God's help, that these adaptations and innovations would allow them to maintain their place on the rapidly expanding frontier of white settlement, even as the United States government came to favor "Indian removal" as a policy for all native peoples east of the Mississippi.

The Wyandot watched as the other tribes in Ohio—the Seneca, Delaware, Shawnee, and Ottawa—left the state for new lands in Kansas and Oklahoma, in large part due to US government pressure. But the Wyandot held out. Then in 1841, Chief Summundewat, Methodist convert and lay preacher, was murdered by two white men while on a hunting trip outside of the Grand Reserve. If someone like him who had done so much to forge a new path between Wyandot tradition and white culture could be murdered in cold blood by white settlers, what hope was there for the tribe in Ohio? The Wyandot decided to move west.

The Wyandot took time to make preparations, scouting out new lands in Kansas and arranging their affairs in Ohio. As part of that process, they negotiated with the federal government that the deed for the mission church was to be turned over to the Missionary Society of the Methodist Episcopal Church, to be held in trust for them. Before leaving, the Wyandot reinterred John Stewart's remains next to the Mission Church. Rev. James Wheeler, the Methodist pastor of the Mission Church at the time, preached a farewell sermon at the Mission Church, before he accompanied the Wyandot to their new lands in Kansas. Then on July 12, 1843, the remaining 664 Wyandot left Upper Sandusky, and the chapter of the Wyandot in Ohio, Methodist and non-Methodist, came to an end.[2]

---

2. Margaret Grey Eyes Solomon, a Wyandot woman born in Upper Sandusky, would choose in 1865 to leave her tribe to return to Upper Sandusky, where she lived for many years until dying in 1890. She was thus the last Wyandot to live in Upper Sandusky, though she did so as an individual separated from her tribe.

A Brief History of the Wyandotte since 1843

Although the Wyandot left Ohio in 1843, they did not leave United States history. On the contrary, they would continue to play at times pivotal roles, and their stories would intersect at many points with the stories of the United States as a whole.

●●●

Photo: Jennifer Silver, Global Ministries

"It's a great honor to be with you this evening, and to bring to each of you the warmest of greetings from the Wyandot Nation of Kansas. The story of our families and their journey of faith is our gift of hope and encouragement for those whose experiences echo ours. . . . Wyandot communities have been repeatedly dispersed; but not destroyed. John Stewart understood the pain of disenfranchisement when he accepted the grace of Jesus. He accepted the call to share the Gospel and joined the Wyandots of Upper Sandusky in 1816. . . . At a time when conflict, political chaos, economic exploitation, violence, and disease are impacting millions of our brothers and sisters around the world, we are reminded that the simple act of identifying the marginalized and widening the circle of inclusion can be a powerful force for positive change. Wyandot men and women have risen to the challenge to advocate for justice and mercy through the Methodist Church, and we recognize that our cultural world view of interconnection and interdependence mirror the teaching of Jesus.

95

. . . Like many of you and your families, we have chosen the path toward renewed strength, resiliency, and empathy in spite of . . . dispersal and scattering."

—Chief Janith English, Wyandot Nation of Kansas, at the Methodist Mission Bicentennial Conference, Atlanta, April 2019, opening banquet recognition of John Stewart and the Wyandotte

The journey to Kansas was long, and many Wyandot died before they reached their new home at the confluence of the Missouri and Kansas Rivers. In the first year there, many Wyandot succumbed to a terrible epidemic and were buried in what is now called the Huron Indian Cemetery, or formally, the Wyandot National Burying Ground, now designated as a National Historic Landmark. In one of their first acts in this new land, the Wyandot built a new Methodist church building. They then created a town that would later become Kansas City, Kansas. The first state government of Kansas was largely created by Wyandot. Wyandot leaders would be key figures in national debates about slavery and its status in Kansas. Through it all, the Wyandot continued to succeed in forging a future for themselves.

But Wyandot success once again drew white covetousness. The Mississippi River proved to be an ineffective barrier at keeping white settlers away from native lands, and US federal policies continued to support white settlers in their drive to expropriate native lands. In 1855, a group of Wyandot ceded their federally recognized tribal membership in exchange for US citizenship, and in 1867, those who retained their tribal membership again moved, this time to Oklahoma, where they eventually became the federally recognized Wyandotte Nation of Oklahoma. The descendants of those who chose US citizenship and remained in Kansas are today the Wyandot Nation of Kansas, though at present this group is not federally recognized.

The cultural, economic, and political pressures of surrounding white settlers and the US government would weigh heavily on both groups of Wyandottes throughout much of the twentieth century, as they did on other native groups. But starting in the 1980s, there were increasing efforts by native peoples, including Wyandotte, to reclaim and renew their cultures. For the Wyandotte Nation of Oklahoma, these efforts included pow wows, historical committees to recover and retell the stories of their past, and an education center to celebrate their culture. Similar efforts to renew a sense of native identity happened among the Wyandot Nation of Kansas and the Wyandot of Anderdon Nation in Michigan, descendants of a group of Wyandot that remained near Detroit when others moved to the Grand Reserve in Ohio. In 1999, these three groups in the US joined with the Huron Wendat of Lorette in Canada to form the Wendat Confederacy, bringing a reunification of sorts to a group of people separated for well over a century and a half. Representatives of these four groups came together again in 2004 for the first Cultural Week in Wyandotte, Oklahoma.

A Brief History of the Methodists since 1843

Wyandotte Mission Church in disrepair. Circa 1880s.
Photo: GCAH Mission Photograph Album - America #1 page 0122

Wyandotte Mission Church, rebuilt in 1889 under the direction of Rev. N. B. C. Love.
Photo: GCAH Mission Photograph Album - Cities #9 page 0206

While the Wyandotte, including the Methodist Wyandotte, were working to create new lives for themselves in Kansas and Oklahoma, predominantly white Methodists continued to preserve their memory in Ohio. The first white settler congregation was organized in 1845, and it built its own building. The Wyandot Mission Church was not used regularly for services after the departure of the Wyandot, and it fell into disrepair until Rev. N. B. C. Love led an effort to restore it in 1889. Since that restoration effort, the Mission Church building has continued to be owned by the Missionary Society and its successors (now Global Ministries) but maintained by the local Methodist community. By the late twentieth century, Global Ministries was paying for the insurance on the property, but it was (and continues to be) the historic committee of the local congregation that has kept up the property and has worked to share its story with the local community and visitors.

••

"When the Wyandots were forced to leave in 1843, they trusted the Methodists to care for the church and for the graves of their ancestors. . . . In recent years, the Mission Church has been cared for by the Records and History Committee of the John Stewart [United] Methodist Church with the support of the local community. . . . The same committee . . . continues to care for [the Church] today with the full support of the Wyandotte Nation of Oklahoma. As the Wyandottes arrived at the Mission Church for the Land Transfer . . . tears began to fill their eyes. I attempted to greet each one as they stepped off the bus, to welcome them back to the home of their ancestors. Chief Billy Friend, in his comments at the Land Transfer, assured the community that the reason the church was still standing was due to the care and support of the local community and the Records and History Committee. The relationship between the Wyandot and the local community in those early years has come full circle. . . . The true history will continue to be taught at the Wyandot Mission Church. The transfer of the land back to the Wyandottes was also a return of honor, respect, and trust between two peoples."

—*Pastor Betsy Bowen, John Stewart United Methodist Church*

••

Nationally, predominantly white Methodists seemed to forget the close relationships they had with the Wyandot and had aspired to have with other native peoples. Repeatedly, white Methodist clergy and laity sided with white American interests against Native Americans. A Methodist mission to Oregon that was initially intended as a mission to natives soon became a basis for a growing white settler colony that expropriated native lands. Although Methodist ministers worked under Wyandot leadership to create the Wyandot school in Upper Sandusky, later mission schools run by Methodists for native peoples sought to exterminate native culture, not preserve it. Perhaps the worst instance of Methodist complicity in tragedies against native peoples was the Sand Creek Massacre, in which a Methodist preacher, Col. John Chivington, led soldiers who killed hundreds of Cheyenne and Arapaho, most of them women and children. Methodist laity serving as government leaders of Colorado, where the massacre happened, and Methodist clergy in Denver largely abetted the massacre.

Yet the memory of John Stewart and the Wyandot was not erased. It lived on in Upper Sandusky, but the story was retold elsewhere, too. In 1916, there was a commemoration of John Stewart's arrival. The local congregation was renamed from First Methodist Episcopal Church to John Stewart Methodist Episcopal Church (now John Stewart UMC).[3] The large red stone marker that now stands next to Stewart's grave was placed there at that time. In 1919, the Methodist Episcopal Church and Methodist Episcopal Church, South, celebrated the Mission Centenary, a commemoration of one hundred years since the founding of the Missionary Society. That celebration included a three-week-long "world's fair" of Methodist mission in Columbus, Ohio. Associated with that event, thousands of African American Methodists made a one-day pilgrimage to Upper Sandusky to commemorate the role that John Stewart, a black man, had in starting Methodist mission. Again, in 1960, The Methodist Church recognized Stewart and the Wyandot when they declared the Wyandot Mission Church to be a Methodist Heritage Site. A sign noting that designation still stands near the church.

By the turn of the twenty-first century, The United Methodist Church as a whole was beginning to acknowledge its past misdeeds against native peoples around the United States and to seek closer relationships with them. In 1992, the General Conference adopted a "Confession to Native Americans." Similar resolutions followed in subsequent years. In 1996, the UMC began to take steps to atone for Methodists' role in the Sand Creek Massacre, culminating in an Act of Repentance at the 2016 General Conference. Acts of Repentance related to other aspects of Methodist relationships with native peoples have become common in various parts of the denomination following the 2012 General Conference Act of Repentance to Indigenous People.

---

3. "History of John Stewart United Methodist Church," John Stewart United Methodist Church, http://www.johnstewartumc.com/history.html, accessed August 7, 2020.

Reestablishing Relationships

By the middle of the 2000s, the increasing drive by the Wyandotte to claim and celebrate their heritage and the ongoing work of United Methodists in Upper Sandusky to preserve the local history of the Wyandot and the Mission Church would bring the two groups together. In 2007, leaders of the Wyandotte Nation of Oklahoma brought a group of Wyandotte school children to Upper Sandusky for a historical and cultural learning experience. This trip was the start of yearly visits by the Wyandotte to Upper Sandusky. Through the network established by the Wendat Confederacy, invitations were extended to the Wyandot Nation of Kansas and the Wyandot of Anderdon Nation, who have also sent members to Upper Sandusky to learn about and celebrate Wyandot history there.

Photo: Jennifer Silver, Global Ministries

"The Wyandotte story is simply one of adaptation and perseverance. . . . When John Stewart came to our people in Upper Sandusky, it was a very tumultuous time for us. We had just lost one of our great chiefs. . . . And so when John Stewart came and began to preach the gospel, it was one of the turning-points in our nation's history, in our tribal nation's history. . . . In 2007, we began to take busloads of our kids every summer up to the old Mission Church in Upper Sandusky. . . . On their nametags, it'll have their name today, but it'll also have the name that they trace back to and their ancestor's name. And so, when they go to that church and that mission and that cemetery, they look, and they begin to see that name that's on their nametag. And you begin to see a light go off. And they begin to make a connection with their past. . . . John Stewart and the Methodist mission program—if it wasn't for that church, if it wasn't for that time in our history, we wouldn't be the nation that we are today."

—*Chief Billy Friend, Wyandotte Nation of Oklahoma, at the Methodist Mission Bicentennial Conference, Atlanta, April 2019, opening banquet recognition of John Stewart and the Wyandotte*

• •

The visits by Wyandotte tribal members have also led to renewed opportunities for the predominantly white community of Upper Sandusky to learn more about its history as well. The school district has invited Wyandotte leaders and local historians to present about Wyandotte language, culture, and history to students in the Upper Sandusky schools. The community of Upper Sandusky has taken an increased interest and pride in this part of their community's history.

In the process, close relationships have formed between Wyandotte leaders from all three groups in the United States and local leaders in Upper Sandusky, especially those from the John Stewart United Methodist Church. Thus, in 2016, Wyandotte from Oklahoma, Kansas, and Michigan joined with John Stewart United Methodist Church members and others from the Upper Sandusky community to celebrate 200 years since John Stewart's coming to the Wyandot.

Rev. Brian Arnold, pastor at that point of John Stewart UMC, reached out to Global Ministries to share information about the celebration because of the historic connection of the work of Stewart and the Wyandot with Global Ministries' predecessor, the Missionary Society. This point of contact came just as two initiatives were getting underway at Global Ministries. One was planning for the celebration of Global Ministries' own 200th anniversary, and the other was a review of the properties that Global Ministries owned around the world and an attempt to return them to their original owners. Rev. Arnold's overture was a welcome opportunity for Global Ministries to pursue both of these initiatives in a meaningful new way.

Thus, in the fall of 2018, Thomas Kemper, General Secretary of Global Ministries, Rev. Fred Day, General Secretary of the General Commission on Archives and History, Dr. David W. Scott of Global Ministries, and Steve Movsesian of Global Ministries traveled to Upper Sandusky to meet with Chief Billy Friend of the Wyandotte Nation of Oklahoma, Chief Ted Roll of the Wyandot of Anderdon Nation, Pastor Betsy Bowen and Rev. Brian Arnold of John Stewart UMC, other Wyandotte tribal members, and other members of the Upper Sandusky community. Those present discussed the possibility of returning the Mission Church from Global Ministries to the Wyandotte Nation of Oklahoma.

· ·

"I first met Chief Billy Friend in September of 2012 in Wyandotte, Oklahoma at their yearly Pow Wow and Cultural Week. . . . It was a visit that has changed my life. . . . Since that time, we have formed strong personal and Tribal relationships, friendships, and partnerships. . . . In October of 2012, Chief Billy made his first trip to Michigan and . . . has been the supporter he said he would be. . . . When we went to Ohio, the first thing he did was to take me to the Mission Church. . . . It was again a life changing experience to be in a place that our ancestors built and worshiped. What a sense of peace! Chief Billy introduced me, not just to the Mission Church but also to the parishioners of the John Stewart United Methodist Church. The relationships, friendships, and partnerships that have been built over the years . . . have added a new perspective to my life. . . . Taking part in the Land Transfer . . . was amazing. The celebration at the Mission Church, when Thomas Kemper passed the deed over to Chief Billy, marked another great accomplishment in both of our histories. The presentation and passing of Wampum Belts, the 'Wyandot Methodist Church Return Belt' and the 'Wyandot Methodist Church Cemetery Belt . . . was an inspirational sight to see by all."

—*Chief Ted Roll, Wyandot of Anderdon Nation*

· ·

As Global Ministries came to understand the importance of the story of John Stewart and the Wyandot for its own history, and as plans for the land return proceeded, Global Ministries invited Chief Billy Friend of the Wyandotte Nation of Oklahoma and Chief Janith English of the Wyandot Nation of Kansas to be honored guests at the Methodist Mission Bicentennial Conference in Atlanta in April 2019. The opening banquet of that conference featured both these chiefs, Rev. Day, James Salley, and Rev. Dr. Arun W. Jones, all reflecting on the importance of the connection between the Methodists and the Wyandotte made possible by John Stewart.

The Return of the Mission Church

Photo: Anthony Trueheart, Global Ministries

On September 21, 2019, Wyandotte people, people called (United) Methodist, and the people of the Upper Sandusky community came together to celebrate the formal transfer of ownership of the Wyandot Mission Church, a portion of the surrounding cemetery, and an additional cemetery plot near the river to its rightful owners, the Wyandotte people. An overview of the schedule of events for that day is included in appendix F. It was a significant event for the Wyandotte, for the local community, and for United Methodists across the state of Ohio and around the world. Wyandotte chiefs, singers, dancers, and color guard members participated. Methodist bishops, ministers, and agency executives were present. Local elected leaders and many members of the local community were in attendance. Representatives from two different branches of John Stewart's family were there as well.[4] Over 200 years after John Stewart, the Wyandot, and Methodist clergy came together to start an epic story, the descendants of each of these groups were there to celebrate a new chapter.

---

4. John Stewart married but never had children himself. His siblings, however, did have children, and these branches of the Stewart family continue to celebrate their family's heritage and accomplishments (which extend far beyond those of John).

∙∙∙

"The Historical and Records Committee of the John Stewart United Methodist Church . . . has taken care of this property for so many years. You've heard earlier today about all the different ones that have been involved. I just want to say that it is a miracle that the church is standing, and in the shape that it is in today. And that's a testament to this local community and to this group and their dedication and commitment to preserving not only their history but preserving our history for us. So, I want to thank them for all that they've done. . . . [With this land return] . . . we've established a relationship once again, that relationship with the Methodist Church, that had been established so many years ago; we rekindled that relationship and we began to build once again, that trust between one another. . . . This will always be our church. When I say 'our' I mean 'ours.' It's our church as the Wyandotte people and the Methodist Church. This will be ours together."

—Chief Billy Friend, Wyandotte Nation of Oklahoma, on receiving the title to the Wyandot Mission Church, Upper Sandusky, Ohio, September 21, 2019

∙∙∙

It could be described as nothing less than a sacred moment as this group came together to tell again the story of the Wyandotte and the Methodists over the past two centuries. There was admiration in hearing again of John Stewart and the Wyandot with whom he worked. There was pain in the recounting of the departure of the Wyandot from Upper Sandusky. There was gratitude in recognizing the work of local Methodists in preserving the Mission Church. There was grief in acknowledging the ways that Methodists nationally had sinned against native peoples. There was pride in acknowledging the history of Wyandotte perseverance and the beauty of Wyandotte culture. There was celebration in the return of the land. There was love and friendship in acknowledging the relationships that had made the day possible. This day was a new story that will continue to be told in the years to come.

Lessons from This History

As Global Ministries has reflected on these stories, it has drawn four lessons from them. First, the story is never over. At many times between 1843 and 2019, it would have been difficult to believe that the Mission Church would ever be returned to the Wyandotte. It must have seemed like that story ended in 1843. But 176 years after the Wyandot entrusted it to the Methodists in the faith that they would take care of it, the church was returned. God continues to surprise us by bringing about new things that cannot be imagined beforehand (Eph 3:20).

"As the resident Pastor appointed to John Stewart UM Church in Upper Sandusky, Ohio, I was in part given responsibilities to assist in the oversight of the Wyandot Mission Church property. This was a most unusual experience. . . . My community of responsibility extended half-way across the country to Wyandotte Nation, Wyandotte, Oklahoma. I found myself learning about a culture, not steeped in the western European 'individualism,' but formed by values of collectivism. Individuals are important and valued, so I learned of Wyandot culture, but only as a part of the collective community. . . . The day that the Wyandot Mission Church property was returned . . . brought tears to my eyes several times as I realized that the land was being received, not from an attitude of righteous indignation, but in an attitude of celebration for having become an enlarged community—an enlarged tribe, so to speak. The frequent call for the day was for the emergence of a new community—not Wyandotte and United Methodist, but as a people who experience and stand under the Spirit of one creator, enriching the emerging and future community with a rich, diverse, and generous collective of individuals poised to make the world a better place for all."

—*Rev. Brian E. Arnold, former pastor of John Stewart United Methodist Church*

Second, one cannot draw an easy line between Wyandotte and Methodist—they are mixed together in a way that cannot be separated into clearly distinct groups. Wyandotte history is Methodist history; Methodist history is Wyandotte history. Some Wyandottes are and have been Methodist; some Methodists are and have been Wyandotte. There continue to be close bonds between individuals who are part of both groups, and both groups are part of a larger community.

The third lesson is the importance of friendship. The deed by which the Wyandot gave the Mission Church to the Missionary Society says, "We have buried friends here." Friendship is a large part of what made this place a sacred space. And it was the resumption of friendships between the Wyandotte and the Upper Sandusky community that made the return possible. In his remarks at the land return, Chief Billy Friend said to Betsy Bowen and other members of John Stewart UMC, "I said Betsy, this will always be *our* church. When I say 'our' I mean 'ours.' It's our church as the Wyandotte people and the Methodist Church. This will be ours *together*." What better testimony could there be to friendship and collaboration?

Photo: Anthony Trueheart, Global Ministries

"'We have buried friends here,' the Wyandottes said in the deed in 1843, when they gave these burial grounds to the Methodist Church and the Methodist Missionary Society. Now from this Holy Ground arises renewed friendship between the Wyandotte and the people called Methodist, to walk together into a future of shared experience, respect, and growing friendship."

—Thomas Kemper, General Secretary, Global Ministries, on handing over the title to the Wyandot Mission Church to the Wyandotte, Upper Sandusky, Ohio, September 21, 2019

The final lesson is the importance of telling the story. The moment of joy and of justice that came in the land return was possible because people had kept stories alive. People among the Wyandotte, people in Upper Sandusky, and people in the (United) Methodist connection kept the stories of John Stewart and the Wyandot alive for two centuries. This was not always easy, and at times, not many were interested in hearing them. But there were always at least a faithful few who kept telling the stories, confident that they would one day again be recognized and celebrated for what they were—precious testimonies to the goodness of God.

On the day after the land return ceremony, the Wyandotte did something they had not done in 176 years—they had a church service at their Mission Church. They did so to celebrate and retell the story of their people. And they did so, as the hymn says, "to tell the old, old story of Jesus and his love." One might add that when "in scenes of glory," we gather together—Wyandotte,

Methodists, and all God's people—"to sing the new, new song," we will discover that this song is none other than these old stories of love, relationship, and the wondrous, unexpected things that are possible through God's grace.[5]

Recommended Readings

For more on the history of the Wyandot in Ohio, including their connection to Methodism, see:

- James B. Finley. *History of the Wyandott Mission at Upper Sandusky, Ohio, under the Direction of the Methodist Episcopal Church.* Cincinnati: E. P. Thompson, 1840. https://archive.org /details/historyofwyandot00finl.

- Thelma R. Marsh. *Moccasin Trails to the Cross: A History of the Mission to the Wyandott Indians on the Sandusky Plains.* Upper Sandusky, OH: John Stewart United Methodist Church, 1974.

- Mary Stockwell. *The Other Trail of Tears: The Removal of the Ohio Indians.* Yardley, PA: Westholme, 2016.

The websites of both the Wyandotte Nation of Oklahoma and the Wyandot Nation of Kansas are a wealth of historical information about the tribe before, during, and after their time in Ohio. The website of the Wyandotte Nation of Oklahoma was particularly useful in putting together the brief history of the Wyandotte since 1843 included in this chapter:

- Wyandot Nation of Kansas. "Wyandot History." https://www .wyandot.org/history.htm.

- Wyandotte Nation of Oklahoma. "History." https://www .wyandotte-nation.org/culture/history/.

For more on Methodist relationships with Native Americans, see:

- Kathy L. Gilbert and Linda Bloom. "GC2012: Starting Along the Path of Repentance." *United Methodist News Service.* April

---

5. Lyrics from Katherine Hankey, "I Love to Tell the Story," 1866, *United Methodist Hymnal,* #156.

27, 2012. https://www.umnews.org/en/news/gc2012-starting
-along-the-path-of-repentance.

- "Native People and The United Methodist Church." *2016 Book
  of Resolutions* #3321. https://www.umcjustice.org/who-we-are
  /social-principles-and-resolutions/native-people-and-the
  -united-methodist-church-3321.

- Gary L. Roberts. *Massacre at Sand Creek: How Methodists Were
  Involved in an American Tragedy.* Nashville: Abingdon, 2016.

For more on friendship as a missiological principle, see:

- Daryl R. Ireland, David W. Scott, Grace Y. May, and Casely B.
  Essamuah. *Unlikely Friends: How God Uses Boundary-Crossing
  Friendships to Transform the World.* Eugene, OR: Pickwick,
  forthcoming in 2021.

- Dana L. Robert. *Faithful Friendships: Embracing Diversity in
  Christian Community.* Grand Rapids: William B. Eerdmans,
  2019.

EPILOGUE
ENDURING TENSIONS IN MISSION

Thomas Kemper

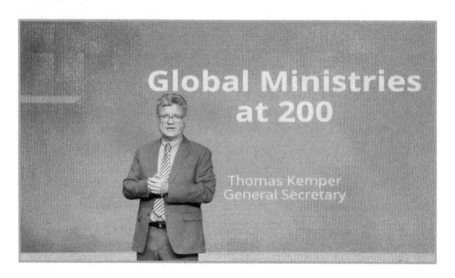

Thomas Kemper at the 2018 Mission Ambassadors Summit, Atlanta, Georgia
Photo: Anthony Trueheart, Global Ministries

This book explored tensions in mission throughout. The tensions are very complicated; mistakes are made, and tensions do arise. In fact, tension is important in mission. It is healthy. It is necessary. Tension exists because this world is not the kin(g)dom of God—not yet. As Christians, we are still waiting for it. And as we move toward that vision of the kin(g)dom of God, we will live and serve in and with tensions. Here are four tensions that I think are important for us as Methodists at this moment in mission history.

First, there is a tension between what we confess and what we practice. Global Ministries is very clear on its mission theology. It speaks about the *missio Dei*: mission is God's mission. If you ask any mission theologian, she or he will say, "Yes, yes, yes. For the last fifty years, we have seen mission as the *missio Dei*. That is what we believe in."

But too often, we as Christians still practice mission as if it is our mission. This is a tension with which Global Ministries and The United Methodist Church struggle. Too often, humans think we know what mission should look like. We think, "Okay, it's God's mission, but God is so far away." We think we know what is best here and now. We go to some new place and assume we know what to tell people about gospel witness and service, how to teach them and instruct them on the right way forward. Christians constantly wrestle with the tension between the *missio Dei* theology and our inclinations to practice "our mission." We must be humble enough to say, "It is God's mission, not ours," and learn from others how they see God at work in emerging places of mission.

Second, there is tension between God's preferential option for the poor, as expressed in scripture and well developed in the theology of liberation, and the church's de facto richness. At least the church is rich in the global North, and even in many parts of the global South. Not everybody is poor in Africa. There is a lot of wealth on that continent, much of it held by Christians.

We live with this tension, acknowledging that much mission energy comes from the margins but is economically controlled from old mission centers. We talk about "mission from the margins." But the power differential is still from the powerful to the powerless, from the rich to the poor, from the center to the margins, and from those holding prescribed academic education to those who do not have the same type of formal schooling, but who have other forms of life experience and can use that experience to teach those willing to learn. How do we make sense of this tension in day-to-day mission work—that God prefers the poor and looks with compassion upon the poor, yet those who control the formal mission structures are so relatively rich?

Third, there is a tension between incarnation and universal values. There are some values, some gospel convictions that are true everywhere and should be considered and lived out in every part of the world. But then, if the gospel is not contextually incarnated, if the gospel does not take root in every place and according to the reality, the culture, and the people of that place, it becomes meaningless. It becomes just a general idea with no specific appeal. As Eugene Peterson says, it has to move into the neighborhood.[1]

The mission theologian D. T. Niles once said that the gospel comes in a flowerpot.[2] Missionaries, sometimes, have forgotten to destroy the pot so that the roots can really go deep into the soil. They have just brought the pot, so the roots could not go deep in the soil of the locales where they serve. Therefore, Christianity stays something brought in, set on the windowsill, even superficial. We need to be ready to destroy the pot so that the roots can go deep.

Mission involves a constant struggle over values, including those imported by missionaries. I do not want to go into details here because I want to avoid a discussion about controversial issues that I cannot fully explore at the end of this book. Human sexuality is only one such issue. There are so many others that raise questions about the universal aspects of the gospel and contextual expressions. I will dare one example. Global Ministries has struggled with this tension in its efforts to ensure child protection. The agency asks every partner to sign its child protection policy because the leadership and staff strongly believe in it. But the common understanding of child protection in the United States, where the policy originated, differs from that in other parts of the world. How far should the agency adapt its policy to take account of various other perceptions? Does it say, "Our view is the universal value, and you either agree to it or you are out of the mission circle"? It is one example of mission tension.

The fourth tension is the one between the poetry of "from everywhere to everywhere" and the pragmatic considerations of mission implementation. Global Ministries has experienced this tension most dramatically in missionary service. It arose frequently in a consultation Global Ministries organized on such service at Drew Theological School more than a decade ago. Participants talked about guiding principles of missionary service and had a lively

---

1. See John 1:14 in Eugene Peterson, *The Message: The Bible in Contemporary Language* (Colorado Springs, CO: NavPress, 2002).

2. Niles wrote, "It is inevitable that the missionary should bring a pot plant, the Christianity of his own culture; it is essential that he allow the pot to be broken and the plant to be rooted in the soil of the country to which he goes." *That They May Have Life* (New York: Harper & Brothers, 1951), 80–81; quoted in Joon-Sik Park, "The Missionary Theology of D. T. Niles," *International Bulletin of Mission Research* 44, no. 3 (2020): 233–47.

discussion on incarnated living and the practice of a theology of mutuality. We created a beautiful document stating values for missionary service. It has all the right theology. But since then, Global Ministries has struggled with the question of what these values mean when writing the missionary manual. What does incarnate living mean in defining health benefits and pension? What does mutuality mean when weighing the differential between a missionary retiring to India and another retiring to the US? Is the same pension just? Or is it racist if the one retiring to the US gets more pension than the one retiring to India?

What does the agency do with the poetry of mission "from everywhere to everywhere" when some countries do not permit missionaries? When the United States will not allow our two-year young adult Global Mission Fellows to enter the country? When an international airport in Europe denies a transfer permit to a missionary candidate en route to missionary training on another continent?

Suddenly, this very beautiful concept of "from everywhere to everywhere" becomes a big challenge. How should the agency bring it to reality in the real world? It goes on trying because the concept has made Global Ministries special as a mission agency. I think it is one of the very few agencies in the world in which people from over thirty countries are serving. Over 50 percent of its missionaries in 2020 are not from the US but from everywhere to everywhere. The agency wants to continue to grow in this direction—conditions and resources permitting. Yet in the day-to-day, holding it all together and continuing to create equity and justice remains a huge challenge.

I want to leave readers with these four tensions, because I think we cannot be in mission if we do not recognize that mission is messy and filled with tensions. The preceding chapters have shown how tensions have shaped Methodist mission over the last 200 years, and I fully expect tensions to shape mission over the next 200 years as well. My prayer is not that we as Methodists avoid these tensions. We cannot eliminate them because they are healthy, they are important. My prayer is that we may serve faithfully amid them.

PREDECESSOR ORGANIZATIONS OF GLOBAL MINISTRIES

Methodist Episcopal Church

Missionary Society, 1819–1907, divided into Board of Foreign Missions and Board of Home Missions and Church Extension

General Church Extension Society, 1865–1872, replaced by Board of Church Extension

Woman's Foreign Missionary Society, 1869–1939, merged into The Methodist Church

Board of Church Extension, 1872–1907, merged into Board of Home Missions and Church Extension

Woman's Home Missionary Society, 1880–1939, merged into The Methodist Church

Board of Foreign Missions, 1907–1939, merged into The Methodist Church

Board of Home Missions and Church Extension, 1907–1939, merged into The Methodist Church

Wesleyan Service Guild, 1921–1939, merged into The Methodist Church

Methodist Episcopal Church, South

Missionary Society, 1846–1866, divided into Board of Foreign Missions and Board of Domestic Missions

Board of Foreign Missions, 1866–1870, merged into Board of Missions

Board of Domestic Missions, 1866–1870, merged into Board of Missions

Board of Missions, 1870–1939, merged into The Methodist Church

> *Woman's Missionary Council*, 1910–1939, merged into The Methodist Church

Woman's Foreign Missionary Society, 1878–1910, merged into Woman's Missionary Council

General Board of Church Extension, 1882–1939, merged into The Methodist Church

Woman's Parsonage and Home Mission Society, 1890–1910, merged into Woman's Missionary Council

Methodist Protestant Church

Board of Foreign Missions, 1834–1880, renamed to Board of Home and Foreign Missions

Woman's Foreign Missionary Society, 1879–1924, merged into Union Board of Foreign Missionary Administration

Board of Home and Foreign Missions, 1880–1888, divided into Board of Foreign Missions and Board of Home Missions

Board of Foreign Missions, 1888–1924, merged into Union Board of Foreign Missionary Administration

Board of Home Missions, 1888–1928, merged into Board of Missions

Woman's Home Missionary Society, 1893–1907, renamed to Woman's Board of Home Missions

Woman's Board of Home Missions, 1907–1928, merged into Board of Missions

Union Board of Foreign Missionary Administration, 1924–1928, merged into Board of Missions

Board of Missions, 1928–1939, merged into The Methodist Church

The Methodist Church

Board of Missions and Church Extension, 1939–1952, renamed to Board of Missions

Division of Foreign Missions

Division of Home Missions and Church Extension

Woman's Division of Christian Service

Women's Society of Christian Service, 1939–1968, merged into The United Methodist Church

Wesleyan Service Guild, 1939–1968, merged into The United Methodist Church

Board of Missions, 1952–1968, merged into The United Methodist Church

Division of World Missions

Division of National Missions

Woman's Division of Christian Service

Methodist Committee for Overseas Relief (MCOR), 1940–1968, merged into The United Methodist Church

Evangelical Association/United Evangelical Church/Evangelical Church

Missionary Society, 1839–1946, merged into Evangelical United Brethren Church

Board of Missions, 1859–1946, merged into Evangelical United Brethren Church

Woman's Missionary Society, 1930–1946, merged into Evangelical United Brethren Church

Woman's Missionary Society, 1880–1930, merged into Board of Missions

Church Extension Society, 1900–1946, merged into Evangelical United Brethren Church

Christian Service Guild, 1944–1946, merged into EUB Church

Church of the United Brethren in Christ

Missionary Society, 1841–1853, renamed to Home, Frontier, and Foreign Missionary Society

Home, Frontier, and Foreign Missionary Society, 1853–1905, divided into Home Missionary Society and Foreign Missionary Society

Church Erection Society, 1869–1925, merged into The Home Mission and Church Erection Society

Women's Missionary Association, 1874–1909, merged into Foreign Missionary Society

Foreign Missionary Society, 1905–1946, merged into Evangelical United Brethren Church

> *Women's Missionary Association*, 1909–1946, merged into Evangelical United Brethren Church

Home Missionary Society, 1905–1925, merged into The Home Mission and Church Erection Society

The Home Mission and Church Erection Society, 1925–1946, merged into Evangelical United Brethren Church

Evangelical United Brethren Church

Board of Missions, 1946–1968, merged into The United Methodist Church

Women's Society of World Service, 1946–1968, merged into The United Methodist Church

Christian Service Guild, 1946–1958, merged into Women's Society of World Service

The United Methodist Church

Board of Missions, 1968–1972, renamed to Board of Global Ministries

Board of Hospitals and Homes, 1968–1972, merged into Board of Global Ministries

Division of Ecumenical and Interreligious Concerns, 1968–1972, merged into Board of Global Ministries

Women's Society of Christian Service, 1968–1972, merged into United Methodist Women

Wesleyan Service Guild, 1968–1972, merged into United Methodist Women

United Methodist Committee for Overseas Relief (UMCOR), 1968–1972, name changed and merged into Board of Global Ministries

Board of Global Ministries, 1972–1976, renamed to General Board of Global Ministries

> *United Methodist Committee on Relief* (UMCOR), 1972–Present

> *United Methodist Women*, 1972–2012, became independent

General Board of Global Ministries, 1976–Present

> *United Methodist Committee on Relief* (UMCOR), 1972–Present

> *United Methodist Women*, 1972–2012, became independent

Formerly Affiliated, Now Independent

Commission on Ecumenical Concerns and Interreligious Affairs (presently Ecumenical and Interreligious work of the Council of Bishops), became independent in 1980

United Methodist Women, became independent in 2012

GLOBAL MINISTRIES THEOLOGY OF MISSION STATEMENT

The Mission Theology statement guides Global Ministries' participation in the *Missio Dei*. It frames Global Ministries' role within the denominational mission to make disciples of Jesus Christ for the transformation of the world. The transforming power belongs to God, and Global Ministries is in mission to witness to what God has done and is doing, and to learn from what God is doing in every land where disciples gather in the name of Jesus Christ.

God's Mission from Creation to Completion

God's Mission reclaims the life of all creatures and redeems all creation for God's intended purpose. Holy Scriptures bear witness to mission that begins with God, belongs to God, and will be fulfilled by God at the end of time. The Spirit of God, which moved over the waters of chaos at creation, and the Word of God, which became Incarnate in Jesus Christ, leads on to fullness in God's purpose.

The Self-Emptying Life of Jesus the Christ in Service to the Least and the Last

In response to God's Mission for him, Jesus—whom we Christians acknowledge as God's Son, the Christ, the anointed servant of God, and our savior—poured himself out in servanthood for all humanity and emptied himself of divine privilege, assuming the trials and risks of human limitation. Jesus identified in compassion with all humanity and lived in radical faithfulness to the will of God. He became obedient unto death—even a humiliating public execution. In raising Jesus from the dead, God shows willingness and power to reconcile all creation and to restore the world to its divine purpose.

The Church as a Community of Servanthood in Mission

God's Holy Spirit calls the Church into being for mission. The Church is one sign of God's presence in the world and of God's intention for creation. In response to God's call and the leading of the Holy Spirit, women and men, young and old, of all nations, stations, and races, and in all times and places, unite as the living body of Christ to join God's mission of redemption, bearing witness to God's presence in the world. This Community of faith aspires to live out the potential of new life in Christ among all human beings now, while envisioning the fulfillment of God's reign and the completion of God's mission. The Church experiences and engages in God's mission as it pours itself out for others, ready to cross every boundary to call for true human dignity among all peoples, especially among those regarded as the least of God's children, all the while making disciples of Christ for the transformation of the world.

Grace at Work Everywhere

In our Wesleyan tradition we acknowledge the grace of God placed in our hearts and at work in the world before any action on our part. In response we accept and proclaim grace that sets us upon the right path of obedience to the Word made flesh in Jesus Christ. This grace calls us to repentance, and to active faith and good works in Christ. Active faith participates in the perfecting and fulfilling grace of God, which claims and implements the promises of God to deliver exploited persons and oppressed peoples, to restore the sanctity and integrity of God's creation, and to reconcile division in the households of faith and among the peoples and nations of the earth as all of creation groans for redemption. The Wesleyan expectation of "perfection in love" draws redeemed individuals into appropriate, active, transforming relationships of wholeness and unity with God, all people, and creation. Repentance and faith elicit both personal salvation, and social and cosmic transformation.

Transformative Witness

The Church in Mission lifts up the name of Jesus in thought, word, and deed, proclaiming Jesus Christ as "the Word become flesh" through its own incarnate living; deeds of love; and service, healing, and renewal. By representing the revelation of God in Christ in word and deed, the Church remains faithful both to the Great Commandment that we love God with all our heart, soul, mind, and strength, and our neighbor as ourselves; and to the Great Commission that we make disciples of all nations. The Church as faithful community moves full of hope toward the transformation of the world and the day when God's mission is fulfilled.

God's Prior Presence, Our Current Response

God's light shines in every corner of the earth, and God's mission extends to all creation. There are no places where God's grace has not always been present, only places where God in Christ is not recognized, served, or heeded. Because God's image is present in every human being throughout the world, mission partnership embraces witness in all cultures, traditions, political arrangements, economic structures, and languages. Partners in God's mission seek to hear God's voice, to discover the signs of the moving of the Spirit through the world today, and to bear witness to God's activity—overarching past, present, and future—in every local setting.

The Spirit's Surprising Activity

The Spirit is always moving to sweep the Church into a new mission age. With openness and gratitude we await the leading of the Spirit in ways not yet seen as God continues to work God's purposes out in our own day in a new way.

BIOGRAPHICAL POSTERS DISPLAYED AT THE METHODIST MISSION BICENTENNIAL CONFERENCE

The following is a list of individuals, or groups of individuals, whose stories were included in posters displayed at "Answering the Call," the Methodist mission bicentennial conference, Atlanta, April 8–10, 2019. The list is arranged in chronological order, and the appellations are taken from the posters.

Nathan Bangs (1778–1862), First Executive of the Methodist Episcopal Missionary Society

John Stewart (1786–1823), Founder of the First Permanent Methodist Episcopal Mission Among Native Americans

Ann Wilkins (1806–1857), Outstanding Early Missionary to Liberia

Wilhelm Nast (1807–1899), The First German Methodist Missionary

William (1818–1899) and Clementina Rowe (1820–1913) Butler, Founders of American Methodist Missions in India and Mexico

William Taylor (1821–1902), Methodist Episcopal Missionary Bishop, Mission Theorist and Holiness Advocate

James William Lambuth (1830–1892), Mary Isabella McClellan Lambuth (1832–1904), Walter Russell Lambuth (1854–1921), and Nora Kate Lambuth Park (1863–1949), Missionary Family Dynasty

James M. Thoburn (1836–1922) and Isabella Thoburn (1840–1901), Siblings Who Developed New Initiatives in Mission

Amanda Berry Smith (1837–1915), African American Holiness Evangelist and Missionary

Frances Willard (1839–1898), Anna Howard Shaw (1847–1919), and Katharine (Kate) Bushnell (1856–1946), Advocates for New Rights for Women

John Jasper Methvin (1846–1941), Andres Martinez (1855–1935), and Kicking Bird (1863–1935), Missionaries in Kiowa Country

Gertrude Howe (1847–1928), Ida Kahn/Kang Cheng (1873–1930), and Mary Stone/Shi Meiyu (1873–1954), First Female Chinese Doctors and Their Teacher

Francisco Penzotti (1851–1925), Founder of Peruvian Methodism

Lochie Rankin (1851–1929), First Single Woman Missionary of MECS

Marietta Hatfield (1851–1898), Mary C. Archer (1864–1898), and Ella M. Schenck (1866–1898), United Brethren Missionaries and Hospital in Sierra Leone

Susan Angeline Collins (1851–1940), Anna E. Hall (1870–1964), and Martha Drummer (1871–1937), African American Women Led the Way as Missionaries in Africa

Belle Harris Bennett (1852–1922), Mission Organization Leader and Champion for Women's Rights

William Fitzjames Oldham (1854–1937), Methodist Missionary and Bishop in India, Southeast Asia and South America

Henry G. (1858–1902) and Ella Dodge (1854–1916) Appenzeller, Pioneering Methodist Missionaries to Korea

Teikichi Sunamoto (1857–1938), A Founder of Methodism in Japan

Herbert Welch (1862–1969), Mission Bishop and Founder of Relief Agency

John R. Mott (1865–1955), Statesman for Mission and Ecumenism

Anna Eklund (1867–1949), Deaconess Who Served the Poor of Russia

Alma Mathews (1867–1933) and Kathryn Maurer (1881–1962), Ministry to Immigrant Women and Children

Helen Chapman Rasmussen Springer (1868–1946), John McKendree Springer (1873–1963), and Tshangand Kayeke (1880?–19??), Founders of Congolese Methodism

E. Stanley Jones (1884–1973), Missionary to India, Global Evangelist and Author

Justina Lorenz Showers (1885–1984), EUB Mission Leader

Kim Hwal-Lan (Helen Kim) (1899–1970) and Prudencia L. Fabro (1910–1996), Led Mission-Founded Educational Institutions

Ulysses Samuel (U. S.) (1913–2009) and Vivienne Newton (1917–1988) Gray, African American Missionaries to Liberia

J. Harry Haines (1917–2007), Missionary and Relief Agency Director

Mai Gray (1922–2019), A Methodist and an Activist

Theressa Hoover (1925–2013), Groundbreaking Mission Executive

PROGRAM FOR THE METHODIST MISSION BICENTENNIAL BANQUET AND CONFERENCE

Monday, April 8, 2019

2:30 pm–3:30 pm Tour of Global Ministries' Building

5:00 pm Opening Banquet/Plenary Session #1

African Drumming by ConunDrums

Welcome

- Thomas Kemper, General Secretary, Global Ministries, The United Methodist Church

- Dr. Jan Love, Dean, Candler School of Theology, Emory University

- Dr. David W. Scott, Director of Mission Theology, Global Ministries, and Bicentennial Conference Coordinator

Moment of Silence

Native Land Acknowledgment

- The Rev. Glen Chebon Kernell Jr., Executive Director, Native American Comprehensive Plan, Discipleship Ministries

Song: "Our Stories Are Old Stories" Words and Music by Paul Friesen-Carper

Recognition of John Stewart and the Wyandotte people

- The Rev. Alfred T. Day III, General Secretary, General Commission on Archives and History

- Chief Billy Friend, Chief, Wyandotte Nation of Oklahoma

- Chief Janith English, Principal Chief, Wyandot Nation of Kansas

- Mr. James H. Salley, Associate Vice Chancellor, Africa University; Member, Black Methodists for Church Renewal Board of Directors; and Former Director, Global Ministries

Prayer

Hymn: "In Mission Together" Words and Music by S. T. Kimbrough Jr. and Jorge Lockward

Special Greetings

- Bishop Ken Carter, President, Council of Bishops, The United Methodist Church

- Bishop Hee-Soo Jung, President, Global Ministries Board of Directors

- Harriett Olson, General Secretary, United Methodist Women

- The Rev. Dr. Casely Essamuah, Secretary, Global Christian Forum

Medley of Global Songs by the Candler Singers

Scripture: Philippians 4:8–9

Introduction of Speaker

- Dr. Jan Love, Dean, Candler School of Theology, Emory University

Keynote Address: "The Virtues of Mission"

- The Rev. Dr. Arun Jones, Dan and Lillian Hankey Associate Professor of World Evangelism, Candler School of Theology, Emory University, and Bicentennial Steering Committee Member

Hymn: "I Love to Tell the Story" Words by Kate Hankey, Music by William G. Fischer

Closing Remarks

- Thomas Kemper, General Secretary, Global Ministries, The United Methodist Church

Tuesday, April 9, 2019

7:30am–9:00 am United Methodist Professors of Mission Meeting

9:00 am–10:30 am Plenary Session #2

Worship

- Katie Reimer, Conference Worship Leader

Scripture: 2 Corinthians 5:19–21

Introduction of Speaker

- Bishop John Yambasu, Sierra Leone Episcopal Area, The United Methodist Church, and Vice President, Global Ministries Board of Directors

Keynote Address: "Overcoming Wars, Violence, Political, Social and Economic Challenges through Mission: Mission as Peacemaking and Peacebuilding in the North Katanga Area of the Democratic Republic of the Congo"

- Bishop Mande Muyombo, North Katanga Episcopal Area, The United Methodist Church

Questions and Discussion

11:00 am–12:00 pm Small-Group Sharing Session #1

1:30 pm–3:00 pm Breakout Session #1: Milestones in Methodist Mission History

Chair:

- The Rev. Dr. J. Kabamba Kiboko, Lead Pastor, Forest Chapel UMC; President of the African Clergywomen Association; and Bicentennial Steering Committee Member

Presenters:

- "Precursors to Methodist Mission," the Rev. Dr. Benjamin L. Hartley, Associate Professor of Christian Mission, George Fox University

- "The First Women of Theology: Wives, Missionaries, Deaconesses, and the Beginnings of Boston University," Dr. Dana L. Robert, Truman Collins Professor of World Christianity and History of Mission, and Director of the Center for Global Christianity and Mission, Boston University

- "A Methodist World's Fair: The 1919 Centenary Celebration of American Methodist Missions," Dr. Christopher J. Anderson, Special Collections Librarian and Curator of the Day Missions Collection, Divinity Library, Yale University

1:30 pm–3:00 pm Breakout Session #2: Native Americans and Methodist Mission

Chair:

- Thomas Kemper, General Secretary, Global Ministries

Presenters:

- "John Stewart, the Wyandotte, and the Origins of the Missionary Society of the Methodist Episcopal Church," the Rev. Alfred T. Day III, General Secretary, General Commission on Archives and History, and Bicentennial Steering Committee Member

- "Native American Theology and Methodist Mission," the Rev. Glen Chebon Kernell Jr., Executive Director of Native American Comprehensive Plan, Discipleship Ministries

1:30 pm–3:00pm Breakout Session #3: Mission and Migration

Chair:

- Dr. Jehu Hanciles, D. W. and Ruth Brooks Associate Professor of World Christianity, Candler School of Theology, Emory University

Presenters:

- "Methodist Mission to the Anglophone Caribbean and the Role of Their Emancipatory Theology in Mission through Their Migration to the USA," the Rev. Sheryl Marks-Williams, Doctoral Student, Asbury Theological Seminary

- "Methodist Mission and Migration in Germany," the Rev. Walther Seiler, Pastor, Evangelisch-methodistische Kirche-Gemeinde Albstadt

- "Standing in Spiritual and Material Solidarity with Migrants," Bishop Felipe Ruiz Aguilar, Northeast Annual Conference, and President of the General Cabinet, Methodist Church of Mexico

1:30 pm–3:00 pm Breakout Session #4: Mission, Peace and Reconciliation

Chair:

- The Rev. Dr. Anne Burkholder, Associate Dean of Methodist Studies and Professor in the Practice of Ecclesiology and Church Leadership, Candler School of Theology, Emory University

Presenters:

- "Towards Just Reconciliation: The Mission of the Church in Response to Ethnopolitical Violence in Kenya," Dr. Kaberia Isaac Kubai, Lecturer, University of Embu

- "Theology of Reconciliation: American Methodist Missionaries in Okinawa in 1950s," Dr. Mikio Miyagi, Visiting Research

Scholar, Center for Global Christianity and Mission, Boston University School of Theology

- "Ubuntu, Wesleyan Social Holiness, and the Quest for Human Dignity in Contexts of Political Violence," the Rev. Dr. Fulgence Nyengele, Professor of Pastoral Care and Counseling in the Chryst Chair in Pastoral Theology, Methodist Theological School in Ohio

- "That We May Live Together," Bev Abma, Board Director, American Friends of Asian Rural Institute

1:30 pm–3:00 pm Breakout Session #5: Race, Class and Culture in Mission

Chair:

- Dr. Jason Morgan Ward, Acting Professor, Department of History, Emory University

Presenters:

- "White Privilege at Work in the Early Methodist Mission to Liberia: The Story of the Rev. George S. Brown, Early African American Missionary," the Rev. Patricia J. Thompson, Historian, New England Annual Conference

- "Marketing Mountain Missions," the Rev. Mike Feely, Director of Mission Advancement, Henderson Settlement

- "The Mission of Korean Methodist Women in the 1960s: The Pioneers of Cross-Cultural Mission," Younghwa Kim, Doctoral Student, Emory University

1:30 pm–3:00 pm Breakout Session #6: New Mission Work in Contemporary Methodism

Chair:

- The Rev. Dr. Luther J. Oconer, Associate Professor of United Methodist Studies and Director of the Center for Evangelical United Brethren Heritage, United Theological Seminary, and Bicentennial Steering Committee Member

Presenters:

- The Rev. Andrew Lee, Global Missionary, Global Ministries, serving as Country Coordinator in the Methodist Mission in Cambodia

- Kristi Painter, US-2 Missionary, Global Ministries, serving at the Arch Street United Methodist Church in Philadelphia

- Katherine Parker, Global Missionary, Global Ministries, serving as Health and Community Transformation Advisor with the United Mission to Nepal (UMN)

4:00 pm–5:30 pm Breakout Session #7: John Wesley and Mission

Chair:

- The Rev. Alfred T. Day III, General Secretary, General Commission on Archives and History, and Bicentennial Steering Committee Member

Presenters:

- "John Wesley's Doctrine of Prevenient Grace and Its Import for Christian Mission in the Chinese World," the Rev. Chris Payk, Doctoral Student, National Chengchi University

- "Missio Dei and the Means of Grace: A Theology of Participation," the Rev. Dr. David Whitworth, Bishop Cornelius and Dorothye Henderson E. Stanley Jones Assistant Professor of Evangelism and United Methodist Strategic Initiatives Liaison, Gammon Theological Seminary

4:00 pm–5:30 pm Breakout Session #8: Women Organized for Mission

Chair:

- Harriett Olson, General Secretary, United Methodist Women

Presenters:

- "Early Methodist Women Missionaries: Contributions and Legacy," the Rev. Dr. Philip Wingeier-Rayo, Dean, Wesley Theological Seminary

133

- "Women in Mission, United for Change," the Rev. Dr. Ellen J. Blue, Mouzon Biggs Jr. Professor of the History of Christianity and United Methodist Studies, Phillips Seminary

- "United Methodist Women and the General Board of Global Ministries: A Symbiotic and Gendered Story of Continuity and Contingency," Dr. Glory Dharmaraj, Retired Director of Mission Theology, United Methodist Women

- "The Interiority of Methodist Mission: The Case of Women Missionaries and Korean Women," the Rev. Dr. K. Kale Yu, Lead Pastor of Mount Zion UMC, and Adjunct Professor of Christianity, High Point University

4:00 pm–5:30 pm Breakout Session #9: Mission and Education

Chair:

- Dr. Amos Nascimento, Associate General Secretary for Global Education and New Initiatives, General Board of Higher Education and Ministry, and Bicentennial Steering Committee Member

Presenters:

- "To Transform the Midnight Empire of Heathendom: John Dempster and the Missional Origins of Methodist Theological Education," the Rev. Dr. Douglas D. Tzan, Director of the Doctor of Ministry and Course of Study Programs and Assistant Professor of Church History and Mission, Wesley Theological Seminary

- "Protestantism and Education: Interiorization of the International Methodist Mission in Brazilian Southeast in the Late 19th Century," Vitor Queiroz Santos, Instructor, Methodist College in Ribeirão Preto

- "Public Health, Education, and Its Impact on Mission in South Africa," the Rev. Dr. Stephen Hendricks, Education Desk Coordinator, Methodist Church of Southern Africa; Dean of Faculty of Dentistry and Professor of Public Health, Sefako Makgatho Health Sciences University, South Africa; and Executive Director: UMC GBHEM LEaD Regional Hub, South Africa

4:00 pm–5:30 pm Breakout Session #10: Mission as Evangelism, Sponsored by the Foundation for Evangelism

Chair:

- Jane Boatwright Wood, President, Foundation for Evangelism

Presenters:

- "Healing a Fractured Salvation," the Rev. Dr. Mark Teasdale, E. Stanley Jones Associate Professor of Evangelism, Garrett-Evangelical Theological Seminary

- "Why Do People Become Methodist Christians in Russia/ Eurasia?" the Rev. Dr. Sergei Nikolaev, E. Stanley Jones Professor of Evangelism and President, Moscow Theological Seminary

- "Missional Formation in Theological Learning and Curricula," the Rev. Dr. Luis Wesley de Souza, Arthur J. Moore Associate Professor in the Practice of Evangelism, Candler School of Theology, and Director, World Methodist Evangelism Institute (WMEI)

4:00 pm–5:30 pm Breakout Session #11: Colonialism and Empire in Mission

Chair:

- The Rev. Dr. Arun Jones, Dan and Lillian Hankey Associate Professor of World Evangelism, Candler School of Theology, Emory University, and Bicentennial Steering Committee Member

Presenters:

- "Decolonizing Mission Partnerships," the Rev. Taylor Denyer, President, Friendly Planet Missiology

- "Re-clothing the Church: A View to Decolonizing Mission in Fiji," Akanisi Tarabe, Methodist Church in Fiji

- "Paradigm Shift in 21st Century Mission in Post-colonial Africa: Rethinking the Future of The United Methodist

Church in Light of Emerging Challenges," the Rev. Dr. Nelson K. Ngoy, Pastor, Wesley UMC, New York Annual Conference

4:00 pm–5:30 pm Breakout Session #12: United Methodist Volunteers in Mission

Chair:

- Maclane Heward, Doctoral Student, Claremont Graduate University

Presenters:

- Ronda Cordill, UMVIM Coordinator, Western Jurisdiction

- Tammy Kuntz, UMVIM Coordinator, North Central Jurisdiction

- Matt Lacey, UMVIM Coordinator, Southeastern Jurisdiction

- Tom Lank, UMVIM Coordinator, Northeastern Jurisdiction

7:30 pm–9:30 pm Reception, Candler School of Theology

Wednesday, April 10, 2019

9:00 am–10:30 am Plenary Session #3

Worship

- Katie Reimer, Conference Worship Leader

Scripture: Matthew 4:18–22

Introduction of Speaker

- Bishop Sue Haupert-Johnson, North Georgia Annual Conference, and Member, Global Ministries Board of Directors

Keynote Address: "Trauma Informed Evangelism"

- The Rev. Elaine A. Heath, Ph.D., Abbess, the Community at Spring Forest, and Former Dean, Duke Divinity School

Questions and Discussion

11:00 am–12:00 pm Small-Group Sharing Session #2

1:30 pm–3:00 pm Breakout Session #13: Theological Understandings of Mission

Chair:

- The Rev. Dr. Luther J. Oconer, Associate Professor of United Methodist Studies and Director of the Center for Evangelical United Brethren Heritage, United Theological Seminary, and Bicentennial Steering Committee Member

Presenters:

- "UMC Teaching Documents for Mission," the Rev. Dr. Darryl W. Stephens, Director of United Methodist Studies, Lancaster Theological Seminary

- "Missional Formation: Theological Education for Methodist Ecclesial Innovation," the Rev. Dr. Jeffrey Conklin-Miller, E. Stanley Jones Assistant Professor of the Practice of Evangelism and Christian Formation, Duke Divinity School

- "Call of Moana: Oceanic View of Methodist Mission," the Rev. Dr. Carmen C. Manalac-Scheuerman, Global Missionary, Global Ministries, serving as Professor of Practical Theology, Davuilevu Theological College

1:30 pm–3:00 pm Breakout Session #14: African Women and Mission

Chair:

- Dr. Dana L. Robert, Truman Collins Professor of World Christianity and History of Mission and Director of the Center for Global Christianity and Mission, Boston University School of Theology, and Bicentennial Steering Committee Member

Presenters:

- The Rev. Dr. Patience Kisakye, Pastor, Port Gibson, Lyons, and Palmyra UMC, Upper New York Annual Conference

- The Rev. Mariami Bockari, Makeni District Superintendent, Sierra Leone Annual Conference

- Betty Spiwe Katiyo, Lay Member, West Zimbabwe Annual Conference

- The Rev. Jacqueline Ngoy Mwayuma, Administrative Assistant to North Katanga Area Bishop Mande Muyombo

- The Rev. Laura Wanza Nyamai, Pastor, Tazama UMC, Kenya-Ethiopia Annual Conference (in absentia)

1:30 pm–3:00 pm Breakout Session #15: Mission, Health, and Healing

Chair:

- Dr. John Blevins, Associate Research Professor, Hubert Department of Global Health, Emory University

Presenters:

- "Health, Suffering and Healing: A Systematic-Theological Reflection with Special Reference to Ameru Cultural Context," the Rev. Dr. Dorcas Kanana Muketha, Lecturer, Chuka University, Kenya

- "Medicine and the Methodist Mission in Korea," the Rev. Dr. Gunshik Shim, Retired, New York Annual Conference

- "Good Religion and Good Agriculture Go Together: The Case of George Roberts," the Rev. Dr. Rich Darr, Pastor, United Methodist Church of Geneva, Northern Illinois Annual Conference

1:30 pm–3:00 pm Breakout Session #16: Ecumenical Dimensions of Mission

Chair:

- Glenn Kellum, Special Assistant to the General Secretary, Global Ministries, and Bicentennial Steering Committee Member

Presenters:

- "Methodist Mission in France," Dr. Michèle Sigg, Associate Director, Dictionary of African Christian Biography, and Managing Editor, *Journal of African Christian Biography*

- "Camping to Promote Holiness and Missions," Bishop Robert Kipkemoi Lang'at, Africa Gospel Church–Kenya

- "Mission Roundtables in South America: Sharing a Common Mission," Lic. Humberto Shikiya, Founder and Member of Board of CREAS, Former Director General of CREAS

1:30 pm–3:00 pm Breakout Session #17: Methodist Mission and Muslims

Chair:

- The Rev. Dr. Deanna Ferree Womack, Assistant Professor of History of Religions and Multifaith Relations, Candler School of Theology

Presenters:

- "Early Encounters with Islam: Methodist Episcopal Missionaries and Muslims in North India in the 19th Century," Dr. Alan M. Guenther, Assistant Professor of History, Briercrest College and Seminary

- "The Wesleyan Spirit of Mission among Muslims in the Middle East: Its History and Implications," the Rev. Dr. Sam Kim, Assistant Professor of the E. Stanley Jones School of Mission, Asbury Theological Seminary

- "The 20th Century Methodist Mission to the Malays: Faithful Mission at the Complex Boundary of Religious Diversity, Ethnic Rivalry and Political Aspirations," the Rev. Dr. Robert A. Hunt, Director of Global Theological Education and Director of the Center for Evangelism, Perkins School of Theology

1:30 pm–3:00 pm Breakout Session #18: Visions of World Methodism

Chair:

- Dr. David W. Scott, Director of Mission Theology, Global Ministries, and Bicentennial Conference Coordinator

Presenters:

- "The World Our Parish: Interrogating the Wesleyan Heritage, North American Methodism and Mission in 21st Century

Africa," the Rev. Dr. J. Kwabena Asamoah-Gyadu, Ordained Minister of the Methodist Church, Ghana, and President, Trinity Theological Seminary, Legon, Ghana

- "Finding the Future of British Methodist World Mission," the Rev. Dr. Stephen Skuce, Director of Global Relationships, The Methodist Church in Britain

4:00 pm–5:30 pm Plenary Session #4

Closing Worship

- Katie Reimer, Conference Worship Leader

Scriptures: Matthew 10:34, Acts 2:17

Introduction of Speaker

- Hannah Hanson, Director, Young Adult Mission Service, Global Ministries

Youth Address: "Turn _____ Upside Down"

- Joy Eva Bohol, Program Executive for Youth Engagement, World Council of Churches (WCC), and Global Missionary, Global Ministries

Benediction

- Bishop Thomas Bickerton, President, UMCOR, and Chair, Bicentennial Steering Committee

7:30 pm–9:30 pm Closing Reception and Celebration

ATTENDEES AT THE METHODIST MISSION BICENTENNIAL CONFERENCE

Bev Abma, Consultant, Asian Rural Institute

Pereira do Lago Adonias, Presidente do CIEMAL e Presidente Quinta Regiao, CIEMAL e Igreja Metodista-Brasil

Veronica Aguilera, Coordinator, Manos Juntas Mexico

Helen Allen, Chief HR Officer, United Methodist Communications

John "Jack" Amick, Director, Sustainable Development, United Methodist Committee on Relief (UMCOR)

Chris Anderson, Special Collections Librarian and Curator of the Day Mission Collection, Yale Divinity Library

Eric Angel, Senior Manager, Itineration, Global Ministries

Isaura Arez, Interpreter

J. Kwabena Asamoah-Gyadu, President of the Seminary, Trinity Theological Seminary, Accra

Øyvind Aske, General Secretary, Metodistkirkens Misjonsselskap, United Methodist Church in Norway

Edgar Avitia Legarda, Regional Representative, Latin America and the Caribbean, Global Ministries

Paul Bankes, Attorney, Whiteman Bankes and Chebot, LLC

Aida Luz Beltran-Gaetan, Retired, North Georgia Annual Conference, The United Methodist Church

Thomas Bickerton, Bishop, New York Annual Conference, The United Methodist Church

Mary "Mele Faiva Manu" Blagojevich, Real Estate Broker, Lennox Tongan United Methodist Church

Michael Blair, Executive Minister—Church in Mission, United Church of Canada

Linda Bloom, Assistant News Editor, United Methodist News Service

Ellen Blue, Professor, Phillips Theological Seminary

Mariama Seray B. Bockari, District Superintendent, Sierra Leone Annual Conference, and Member, African Clergywomen Organization

Joy Eva Bohol, Program Executive for Youth Engagement, World Council of Churches, and Global Missionary, Global Ministries

Kerri Broussard, Senior Director, Global HR and Organizational Development, Global Ministries

Sonia Brum, Manager for US Missionaries, Global Ministries

Daniel Bruno, Director, Centro Metodista de Estudios Wesleyanos, Iglesia Metodista Argentina

Dan Bryant, Lead Pastor, Lakewood United Methodist Church

Ken Carter, Bishop/President of the Council of Bishops, Florida Annual Conference, The United Methodist Church

Elvira Cazombo, Pastor, Igreja Metodista Unida em Angola

Grace Choi, Missionary in Residence, Global Ministries

Jay Choi, Missionary in Residence, Global Ministries

Chin Chung Chong, Bishop, The Methodist Church in Singapore

Judy Chung, Executive Director of Missionary Service, Global Ministries

Nora Colmenares, Senior Manager, Resource Development, Global Ministries

Jeffrey Conklin-Miller, Assistant Professor, Practice of Evangelism and Christian Formation, and Director, Methodist House of Studies, Duke Divinity School

Shannon Conklin-Miller, Assistant General Secretary, Division of Ordained Ministry, General Board of Higher Education and Ministry

Ronda Cordill, Jurisdiction Coordinator, United Methodist Volunteers in Mission, Western Jurisdiction

Beth Corrie, Associate Professor, Candler School of Theology, Emory University

Timothy Crisler, Director, Global Ministries

Ibrahim Dabo, Director of Enterprise Business Systems, Global Ministries

Rich Darr, Senior Pastor, Geneva United Methodist Church

Richard Daulay, Professor, The Methodist Church Indonesia

Katie Dawson, Clergy, Iowa Annual Conference, and Director, Global Ministries

Alfred Day, General Secretary, General Commission on Archives and History

Luc Delporte, Interpreter

Taylor Denyer, Lead Missiologist, Friendly Planet Missiology

Márcio Divino De Oliveira, Missiology Professor, The Methodist School of Theology in São Paulo, Brazil

L. Wesley De Souza, Arthur J. Moore Associate Professor of Evangelism, Candler School of Theology, Emory University

Luis De Souza Cardoso, Head and Operations Manager for the Latin America and the Caribbean Regional Office, Area Liaison for Latin America and the Caribbean, Global Ministries

Glory Dharmaraj, Retired, Director of Mission Theology, United Methodist Women

Ed English, Retired, Great Plains Annual Conference, The United Methodist Church

Janith English, Principal Chief, Wyandot Nation of Kansas

Evelyn Erbele, Missionary, Western Jurisdiction Mission Advocate, Global Ministries

Walter Erbele, Missionary, Western Jurisdiction Mission Advocate, Global Ministries

Casely Essamuah, Secretary, Global Christian Forum

Christy Eubank, Recruitment and Services Intern, Global Ministries, and Student, Candler School of Theology, Emory University

John Higon Eun, Bishop, Korean Methodist Church

Tom Farley, Director of Development, Global Ministries

Mike Feely, Director of Development, Camp Lookout

Margaret Fenton-Sollof, Executive Secretary, Office of the General Secretary and CEO, Global Ministries

Roland Fernandes, Chief Operating Officer and General Treasurer, Global Ministries

Natalia Ferreira, Interpreter

Neomi Fletcher, Student, Candler School of Theology, Emory University

Belinda Forbes, Acción Médica Cristiana, and Global Missionary, Global Ministries

Melanie Foust, Student, Candler School of Theology, Emory University

Mateus Francisco, Director, CETEO

Everald Galbraith, Connexional Bishop, MCCA (Methodist Church in the Caribbean and the Americas)

Paulo Roberto Garcia, Dean, The Methodist School of Theology in São Paulo, Brazil

Oscar Garza, Director, Global Ministries

Jatin Gill, Student, Gammon—Interdenominational Theological Center

Chan Gillham, Interpreter

Esther Karimi Gitobu, United Methodist Volunteers in Mission (UMVIM) Coordinator/Donor Networking, Methodist Mission in Cambodia, and Global Missionary, Global Ministries

Larry Goodpaster, Bishop-in-Residence, Candler School of Theology, Emory University

Alan Guenther, Assistant Professor of History, Briercrest College and Seminary

James L. Gulley, Retired Missionary and Former Staff Member, Global Ministries

Stephen Gunter, Director of E. Stanley Jones Professorships, The Foundation for Evangelism

Michael Gurick, Senior Director of Finance, Global Ministries

Bill Haddock, Pastor and Mission Interpreter, North Carolina Annual Conference, The United Methodist Church

Jehu Hanciles, Associate Professor of World Christianity, Candler School of Theology, Emory University

Gilbert Hanke, General Secretary/CEO, General Commission on United Methodist Men

Hannah Hanson, Director, Young Adult Mission Service, Global Ministries

Marilyn Harbert, Retired Missionary, Global Ministries

Warren L. Harbert, Retired Missionary, Global Ministries

Dawn Wiggins Hare, General Secretary, General Commission on the Status and Role of Women

Jacqueline Harmon, Student, Candler School of Theology, Emory University

Becky Harrell-Wright, Retired Missionary, Global Ministries

Benjamin Hartley, Associate Professor of Christian Mission, George Fox University

Sue Haupert-Johnson, Bishop, North Georgia Annual Conference, The United Methodist Church

Elaine Heath, Abbess, Community at Spring Forest, and Former Dean, Duke Divinity School

Stephen Hendricks, Education Desk Coordinator, Methodist Church of Southern Africa; Dean of Faculty of Dentistry and Professor of Public Health, Sefako Makgatho Health Sciences University; and Executive Director, General Board of Higher Education and Ministry LEaD Regional Hub South Africa

Maclane Heward, Doctoral Candidate, Claremont Graduate University

Ellen Hoover, Retired Missionary, Global Ministries

Jeff Hoover, Retired Missionary, Global Ministries

Christie House, Senior Editor/Writer, Global Ministries

George Howard, Director, Connectional Engagement, Global Ministries

Sarah Howell, Seminarian in Residence, Global Ministries, and Student, Candler School of Theology, Emory University

Lilian Hunt, Lake Highlands United Methodist Church

Robert Hunt, Director of Global Theological Education, Perkins School of Theology, Southern Methodist University

Stanislas Ilunga Mutombo, Construction Manager, North Katanga Episcopal Area, The United Methodist Church

Barbara Jacobsen, Director, Internal Audit, Global Ministries

Simao Jaime, Head of Higher Education, Igreja Metodista Unida em Moçambique

Pyppa Johnson, Disaster Director, Disaster Ministries, Texas Annual Conference, The United Methodist Church

Arun Jones, Dan and Lillian Hankey Associate Professor of World Evangelism, Candler School of Theology, Emory University

Una Jones, Director, Mission Volunteers, Global Ministries

Hee Soo Jung, Bishop, Wisconsin Annual Conference, The United Methodist Church, and President, Global Ministries

Kenneth Kalichi, Dean of Cabinet, Zambia Annual Conference, The United Methodist Church

Nelson Kalombo Ngoy, Pastor, New York Annual Conference, The United Methodist Church, and Scholar, Researcher University of Birmingham

Dorcas Kanana Muketha, Lecturer, Tharaka University College

Betty Katiyo, Managing Director, BSK Consultancy

Glenn Kellum, Special Assistant, Office of the General Secretary, Global Ministries

Thomas Kemper, General Secretary, Global Ministries

Glen Chebon Kernell, Executive Director, Native American Comprehensive Plan, Discipleship Ministries

Jeanne Kabamba Kiboko, Lead Pastor, Forest Chapel United Methodist Church, and President, African Clergywomen Association

Kim Moon Sik, Representative of Laymen, Korean Methodist Church

Sam Kim, Assistant Professor, Asbury Theological Seminary

Thomas Kim, United Methodist News Service

Younghwa Kim, PhD Student, Emory University

Yves Mukana Kinangwa, Student, Candler School of Theology, Emory University

Patience Kisakye, Pastor, Upper New York Annual Conference, The United Methodist Church

Paul Kong, Asia Regional Representative, Global Ministries

Dan Krause, General Secretary, United Methodist Communications

Mary Ellen Kris, Legal and Program Consultant, Global Ministries

Kaberia Isaac Kubai, Lecturer, University of Embu

Adlene Kufarimai, Director of Missions and Advocacy, North Alabama Annual Conference, The United Methodist Church

Tammy Kuntz, Coordinator, United Methodist Volunteers in Mission (UMVIM), North Central Jurisdiction

Kwak Sang Won, Pastor, Korean Methodist Church

Matt Lacey, Executive Director, United Methodist Volunteers in Mission (UMVIM), Southeastern Jurisdiction

Kepifri Lakoh, Director, Monitoring and Evaluation, Global Ministries

Robert Lang'at, Bishop, Africa Gospel Church, Kenya

Tom Lank, Jurisdictional Coordinator, United Methodist Volunteers in Mission (UMVIM), Northeastern Jurisdiction

Andrew Lee, Country Coordinator of Methodist Mission in Cambodia, and Global Missionary, Global Ministries

Jacob Seung Lee, Interpreter

Lee Min Joon, World Mission Auditor, Korean Methodist Church

Allison Lindsey, Associate Director of Connectional Ministries, South Georgia Annual Conference, The United Methodist Church

Mei Liu, Operations and Project Manager, Global Ministries

Ruhong Liu, Asia Program Association, Global Ministries

Kimberly Lord, Director of Global Operations and Leader Support, General Board of Higher Education and Ministry

Jan Love, Dean, Candler School of Theology, Emory University

Dana Lyles, Director, US Office on Multicultural Ministries, Global Ministries

Steve Maga, Pacific Islander Ministry Plan Consultant, Global Ministries

Celestin Malamba Lohalo, Director, Global Ministries

Cristina Manabat, President, Harris Memorial College

Sheryl Marks-Williams, PhD Student, Asbury Theological Seminary

Angela Zenith Masih, Methodist Church in India

Phillip Silas Masih, Bishop, Methodist Church in India

Kathleen Masters, Manager, Missionary Training and Continuing Education, Global Ministries

Brian Mateer, Chair, Mission Engagement Team, Western North Carolina Annual Conference, The United Methodist Church

Sandra Matoushaya, Missional Engagement Coordinator, Western Pennsylvania Annual Conference, The United Methodist Church

Molly McEntire, Missional Trainer and Volunteer Coordinator, Florida Annual Conference, The United Methodist Church

Adjo Gisele Mel, Sociologist, Le Reservoir de Siloe

David Millsaps, VIM Coordinator, Western North Carolina Annual Conference, The United Methodist Church

Mikio Miyagi, Visiting Research Scholar, Boston University School of Theology

Taeko Miyagi, Part-Time Lecturer, Aoyam Gakuin University

Didier Monga wa Shakapanga, Mission Advocate for the Young Adults Mission Service, Global Ministries

Jennifer Moore, Christian Educator, United Methodist Church in Macedonia, and Global Missionary, Global Ministries

Vienna Mutezo, Connectional Ministries Director and Deputy Administrative Assistant to Bishop, Zimbabwe West Annual Conference, The United Methodist Church

Mande Muyombo, Bishop, North Katanga Episcopal Area, The United Methodist Church

Amos Nascimento, Associate General Secretary, General Board of Higher Education and Ministry

Jean Pierre Ndour, Chairperson of Christian Education and Pastor in Charge of Mbour Church, United Methodist Church in Senegal

Jerome Nedderman, Senior Manager of IT Infrastructure and Property, Global Ministries

Jacqueline Ngoy Mwayuma, Pastor, North Katanga Annual Conference, The United Methodist Church

Nancy Nicolas, Executive Director, Kapatiran Kaunlaran Foundation Inc.

Fiona Nieman, Meeting Planning Manager, General Council on Finance and Administration (GCFA)

Sergei Nikolaev, E. Stanley Jones Professor of Evangelism, Moscow Theological Seminary

Fulgence Nyengele, Professor of Pastoral Care and Counseling, Methodist Theological School in Ohio

Luther Oconer, Associate Professor of United Methodist Studies, United Theological Seminary

Oh Il Young, Missionary Secretary, Korean Methodist Church

Erica Oliveira, Mission Advocate, Young Adult Mission Service, Global Ministries

Harriett Olson, General Secretary/CEO, United Methodist Women

David Ortigoza, Interpreter

Hector F. Ortiz, Bishop, Methodist Church of Puerto Rico

Sotico Pagulayan, Student, Candler School of Theology, Emory University

Kristi Painter, Arch Street United Methodist Church, Philadelphia, and Global Mission Fellow US-2, Global Ministries

Luckmal Panditharathna, Student, McCormick, Theological Seminary

Glenn Roy Paraso, CEO, Mary Johnston Hospital, The United Methodist Church, Philippines Central Conference

Park Jung Min, Pastor, Korean Methodist Church

Park Sang Cheol, President, World Mission Association, Korean Methodist Church

Katherine Parker, Health and Community Transformation Advisor, United Mission to Nepal; Global Missionary, Global Ministries; and Chairperson, United Methodist Missionary Association (UMMA)

Dale Patterson, Archivist, Records Administrator, General Commission on Archives and History

Christopher Payk, Pastor, Free Methodist Church

René Perez, District Superintendent, New England Annual Conference, The United Methodist Church

Kayilu Pfoze, Student, Candler School of Theology, Emory University

Russell Pierce, Executive Director, Mission Engagement, and Director, the Advance, Global Ministries

Hendrik Pieterse, Associate Professor of Global Christianity and World Religions, Garrett Evangelical Theological Seminary

Shari Ponder, Seminarian in Residence, Global Ministries, and Student, Candler School of Theology, Emory University

Vitor Queiroz Santos, Student, São Paulo University

Gail Quigg, Missionary, North Central Jurisdiction Mission Advocate, Global Ministries

Stephen Quigg, Missionary, North Central Jurisdiction Mission Advocate, Global Ministries

Morais Quissico, Interpreter

James Railey, Pastor, St. Paul River Left Bank Churches Association

Donald Reasoner, Director of Interpretation Services, Global Ministries

Dennis Reimer, First United Methodist Church, Neenah/Menasha, Wisconsin, and In Mission Together Partnership, First United Methodist Church, Pilviskiai, Lithuania

Jeanie Reimer, In Mission Together (IMT) Partnership Coordinator for Lithuania/Latvia, Global Ministries

Katie Reimer, Worship Consultant, Global Ministries

Dana Robert, Truman Collins Professor of World Christianity and History of Mission, Boston University School of Theology

Nancy Robinson, Missionary, Southeastern Jurisdiction Mission Advocate, Global Ministries

Lana Robyne, Director, Wesley Foundation at Purdue, and Board Member, Friendly Planet Missiology

Glenn Rowley, Director, Virginia Annual Conference Office of Justice and Missional Excellence

Felipe Ruiz, Bishop, Iglesia Metodista de México, A. R.

Ryu Ho Joon, Elder, Korean Methodist Church

Jerome Sahabandhu, Mission Theologian in Residence, Global Ministries

James Salley, Associate Vice Chancellor for Institutional Advancement, Africa University

Cindy Saufferer, Director, Global Ministries, and Board Secretary, United Methodist Women (UMW)

Carmen Scheuerman, Professor, Davuilevu Theological College, and Global Missionary, Global Ministries

Kristen Schmitz, Retired Missionary, Global Ministries

Larry Schmitz, Retired Missionary, Global Ministries

Marilia Schüller, Secretary for Racial and Gender Equity, KOINONIA Ecumenical Presence and Service, and Global Missionary, Global Ministries

David Scott, Director of Mission Theology, Global Ministries

Izabel Scott, Administrative Assistant, Global Ministries

Walther Seiler, Pastor, The United Methodist Church in Germany

Humberto Shikiya, Senior Advisor, CREAS—Ecumenical Regional Organization for Advisory and Service

Gunshik Shim, Retired Pastor, New York Annual Conference, The United Methodist Church

Michele Sigg, Associate Director, Dictionary of African Christian Biography

Jennifer Silver, Content Producer, Global Ministries

Kristi Wilson Sinurat, Bishop, The Methodist Church Indonesia, Region I

Stephen Skuce, Director of Global Relationships, Methodist Church in Britain

Michael Sluder, Director of Connectional Ministries, Holston Annual Conference, The United Methodist Church

Prescilla Esperanza Soriano, President, Aldersgate College

Andreas Staempfli, Director, Global Ministries

Darryl Stephens, Director of United Methodist Studies, Lancaster Theological Seminary

Üllas Tankler, Regional Representative, Europe, Eurasia, North Africa, and Middle East, Global Ministries

Akanisi Tarabe, Methodist Church of Fiji

Mark Teasdale, E. Stanley Jones Professor of Evangelism, Garrett-Evangelical Theological Seminary

Patricia Thompson, Coordinating Pastor in Charge of Administration, Wolcott United Methodist Church

Sabam Tobing, Bishop, Region 2, The Methodist Church, Indonesia

Carol Toney, Director, Global Ministries

Pedro Torio, Bishop, Baguio Episcopal Area, The United Methodist Church

Anthony Truehart, Videographer, Global Ministries

Blair Trygstad-Stowe, Lead Pastor, First UMC of Ontario/Open Space

Douglas Tzan, Assistant Dean and Director for Doctor of Ministry and Course of Study, and Assistant Professor of Church History and Mission, Wesley Theological Seminary

Amy Valdez Barker, Executive Director, Global Mission Connections, Global Ministries

Abel Vega, Director of Outreach Vitality, Rio Texas Annual Conference, The United Methodist Church

Carmen Vianese, Director, Global Ministries

Wen Ge, Associate General Secretary, China Christian Council

Asti White, Wesley Foundation of Kalamazoo, and Global Mission Fellow, Global Ministries

Jaye White, Director of Outreach Ministries, North Carolina Annual Conference, The United Methodist Church

Lisa Beth White, Consultant, Sister of Hope Ministries

Sara White, Director of Congregational Development, South Carolina Annual Conference, The United Methodist Church

Catherine Whitlatch, Retired Missionary, Global Ministries

Ron Whitlatch, Retired Missionary, Global Ministries

David Whitworth, Bishop Cornelius and Dorothye Henderson Chair and E. Stanley Jones Assistant Professor of Evangelism, Gammon Theological Seminary—Interdenominational Theological Center

Tahir Widjaja, President of the Provisional Annual Conference, The Methodist Church, Indonesia

David Wilson, Conference Superintendent, Oklahoma Indian Missionary Conference, and Director, Global Ministries

Jim Wilson, St. Paul's United Methodist Church, Tulsa, Oklahoma

Doug Wingeier, Emeritus Professor of Practical Theology, Garrett-Evangelical Theological Seminary, and Retired Missionary, Global Ministries

Philip Wingeier-Rayo, Dean and Professor of Missiology and Methodist Studies, Wesley Theological Seminary

Deanna Womack, Assistant Professor of History of Religions and Multifaith Relations, Candler School of Theology, Emory University

Gordon Wong, President, Trinity Annual Conference, Methodist Church in Singapore

Jane Wood, President, The Foundation for Evangelism

Elliott Wright, Communications Consultant, Global Ministries

Jim Wright, Retired, Rio Texas Annual Conference, The United Methodist Church

David C. Wu, Retired Missionary, Global Ministries

Shirley Wu, Retired Missionary, Global Ministries

John Yambasu, Bishop, Sierra Leone Annual Conference, The United Methodist Church

Yollande Yambo, Africa Regional Representative, Global Ministries

Jae Hyung Yoon, Missionary, Interserve

K. Kale Yu, Adjunct Professor, High Point University

Christy Bulus Yusuf, Director, The United Methodist Church of Nigeria

PROGRAM FOR THE RETURN OF WYANDOTTE LAND

A Remembrance of Our Shared History: The Wyandotte/Wyandot and the People Called Methodists

Saturday, September 21, 2019

Upper Sandusky, Ohio

Program

Call to Worship

Opening Prayer

Land Acknowledgment

Welcome and Introductions

The Lord's Prayer

An Invitation to the Procession

Procession to Burial Grounds and Mission Church

Land Acknowledgment

Telling of the Story

Pipe Ceremony

A Time of Remembrance

Transfer of Land

Statement from the Wyandotte Nation

Dancing

Sending Forth

Celebration Dinner at John Stewart UMC

CPSIA information can be obtained
at www.ICGtesting.com
Printed in the USA
LVHW052150090121
676015LV00005B/7

9 781791 015985